The Vibrant Caribbean Pot

100 Traditional and Fusion Recipes

Vol. 2

ISBN:
978-0-9920505-0-4

First Published in 2014

Prop and food styling/food photography: Chris De La Rosa
Cover and biography pictures: Rohan Laylor of phatdogvisuals.com
Editor: Izabela Szydlo
Art director: Ashley McKenzie-Barnes of vividbeautydesigns.com
Project manager: Karen Nicole Smith

Publisher: Del Media
2-558 Upper Gage Ave Suite 225
Hamilton, Ontario L8V 4J6 Canada

For all inquires, please contact us at CaribbeanPot.com
Phone: 1.347.379.1969

Produced by Formosa Labs
Printed in China

Dedication

This book is dedicated to my mom and dad, Rookmin and Joseph De La Rosa.

*t*he vast collection of islands—more than 7,000 to be exact—that makes up the Caribbean has a lot to offer. The islands are surrounded by crystal clear seas, and have picturesque white-sand beaches, lush jungles and awe-worthy sites that make them tourist hot spots. They have fostered impressive names such as Bob Marley, Stokely Carmichael, Sidney Poitier, and more recently Rihanna, Usain Bolt and Nicki Minaj. Then there's the music. The sweet sounds of soca, chutney, reggae, dancehall, steel pan, calypso, zouk, and more further enhance the atmosphere of the islands.

But none of this would be complete without Caribbean cuisine. A combination of African, Amerindian, European, East Indian, Middle Eastern and Chinese, it is the ultimate fusion of traditions brought from the homelands of the region's population. From the most famous dishes such as Jamaican Jerk Chicken to lesser-known delicacies such as Grenada's Oil Down, variety is the main ingredient of Caribbean fare.

It is this variety that Chris De La Rosa serves up in the follow-up to his e-cookbook, The Vibrant Caribbean Pot: 60 Traditional and Fusion Recipes Vol. 1. Born in Trinidad and Tobago, and now based in Hamilton, Ontario, Canada, the self-taught chef has not only mastered traditional and fusion dishes. He has also become an expert who flows effortlessly from simmering pots of Guyanese Pepperpot and Trinidadian Pelau to sizzling pans of Jamaican Fried Dumplings and more. But, of course, like other foodies, Chris has a foundation for his culinary skills—and it happens to be a solid one. Growing up in a small village, where his family cooked with herbs and spices from its own garden, Chris was groomed in the kitchen by his grandmothers, parents, uncles and aunts. The foundation has established Chris' site, CaribbeanPot.com, as the go-to online hub for Caribbean cooking.

And it is with the same base in mind that he handpicked the 100 recipes in The Vibrant Caribbean Pot Vol. 2, his debut printed release in what will be a series of cookbooks. Easy-to-follow directions that have seen CaribbeanPot.com visited by millions—from the Isle of Man to Lithuania and beyond—and Chris' consideration of accessible ingredients guarantee you will master every lip-smacking dish in the book.

But what truly sets The Vibrant Caribbean Pot apart from any other cookbook is Chris' passion for promoting the appeal of Caribbean fare to the level of France's haute cuisine and Italy's comforting pasta choices. It is time that dishes such as Callaloo and Pikliz become household names and Chris De La Rosa, with his simple, down-to-earth and enthusiastic approach to the Caribbean kitchen, is just the person to make that happen.

So, flip through these pages, fire up your stove, barbecue or oven, turn on your favourite Caribbean tunes and, from the comfort of your own kitchen, take a culinary journey like no other.

Izabela Szydlo

*National Food & Wellness Editor, Metro English Canada
(Canada's most read daily paper)*

*i*t's around one a.m. and I'm about 30,000 feet in the air, desperately trying to get comfortable in this confining airplane seat. Is this how sardines in a tin feel? After a four-hour wait and a narrow escape from a nasty winter storm, my family is on its way to Port of Spain, Trinidad and Tobago—home! There's extreme excitement, as we planned this trip to coincide with Carnival. But it is also thrilling because it's a homecoming that showcases the culinary journey I embarked on many years ago as a little boy, in a little village, on a little island. I've come full circle!

In the weeks leading up to our trip, all I could do was reminisce about the culinary delights I enjoyed as a youth and try my best to retrace, in my mind, the steps to finding good street food. "Is my favourite Doubles man still at the same location?" I wondered. "Will the Bake and Shark sandwiches at Maracas Bay still have that delightful garlic sauce? Can my stomach still handle the zesty Black Pudding from Charlie's in San Fernando?" The thought of eating a few slices of Black Pudding on a Hops bread (like a large dinner roll) drizzled with wicked pepper sauce had me salivating.

My appreciation for Caribbean food started when I was very young and would accompany my mom to the market to shop for produce, salted and smoked meats, and fish, then help her in the kitchen. She didn't buy frozen meats, so the chicken, pork and beef we ate usually came from farmers closer to home. The sights, sounds and scents of the market have remained with me all these years. The fresh produce, the ladies in their colourful dresses, the wicker shopping baskets and the overall vibe of people haggling away at prices—that's the type of vibrancy I've missed the past twenty-two years since moving to Canada. I can still hear vendors shouting out,"Only two dollas ah pong!" (only two dollars a pound), to attract customers. If you've ever been to a Caribbean market, you'll know that there's also a corner (especially later in the day) where the scent is "ripe" and you take small breaths or try your best not to breathe as you walk by. I wonder if this

is the reason my brother and sisters were never as excited as I to go with mom to the market.

Looking back, I also realize why my dad always had my siblings and I in the kitchen garden with him. Unknowingly, we were learning where the food came from. As a result, our mom didn't have to say, "Doh waste that food eh" (don't waste that food) because we knew how much work went into our meals before they reached the table. Although as a youth I'd find any excuse possible not to accompany dad (cricket and soccer seemed so much more important), now I purposely visit my parents during the summer months so dad can show me what he's growing in his tiny garden. After all these years, the man can still teach me a thing or two and is always excited to do so!

Since I went to primary and then secondary school in the city (about one hour away from home), I left my sleepy village early in the morning and returned at dusk. The only free time I had was on the weekends, which I looked forward to because they meant going fishing with my Uncle B. We would cook whatever we caught and the times we came home empty-handed, he would improvise by making a massive pot of soup—thick with ground provisions and flavoured with salted meats.

Meanwhile, during the summer days, life was all about hooking up with friends for "bush cooks". These consisted of taking a pot and ingredients into the forest and putting together a meal. While rustic, cooking over an open flame and being outdoors added to the appeal of it all. These "bush cooks" not only meant good food, but also being with friends, sharing jokes and enjoying life as a teenager.

When summer ended, secondary school days were filled with food vendors who sold a variety of street food just outside of the school's gate. Indian delicacies like Saheena, Doubles, Pholourie and Aloo Pie, all topped with mango chutney or spicy tamarind sauce, were common. Other vendors sold sandwiches with cheese, curry channa (chickpeas) or stewed meats. If you had money left, you'd finish off with spicy preserves like red mango, plum or cherry—the hotter the better!

Returning to the simplicity of village life after school always put things in perspective. If you passed a village elder and did not greet him or her, you'd pay for it with a serious tongue-lashing (and most likely a real "lashing") when your parents found out. The community feel was especially evident during religious holidays. You were always invited to neighbours' homes, even if you didn't observe a particular religion. It wasn't strange for us to celebrate Divali, Eid, Christmas and everything in between with our neighbours. These holidays included an array of food and I always looked forward to Divali for the mass of curry dishes and various sweets.

But it's Christmas on the islands that is unlike anything you've ever experienced. It actually isn't about the gifts (seriously) but instead about food, music and good times. Parang is in the air, the house smells like fresh paint, new curtains are hung and the aroma coming out of the kitchen is heavenly. There is always an extensive menu of Black Cake, Pasteles, baked pork, roasted chicken, stewed peas and beans, Pelau, stewed pork and ground provisions. This type of spread is the norm everywhere you go as you visit family and friends to partake in the culinary delights. How I miss Sorrel made from fresh flower petals rather than the dried ones I now get in Canada.

It's safe to say I was surrounded by food from early on and everyone around me—from my mom and dad to uncles, aunts, friends and cousins—can all handle themselves in the kitchen. My grandmothers were exceptional cooks and right up until they passed, both schooled me if I gave them the chance. Cooking came naturally to my family so when I hear people say that they can't cook, it's a bit difficult for me to digest.

Moving to Canada was a rude awakening. It wasn't just the climate, not having friends or everything moving at a faster speed that made the transition difficult. Getting the produce we would normally use at home was not easy in those days, so the kitchen was not as friendly as I'd remembered. The Caribbean community in Hamilton, Ontario was very small, so we didn't have buying power to demand the things we needed to make the kitchen feel like home. As new immigrants typically do, my aunt worked long hours. So, it was up to my younger cousins and I to work the kitchen. After an overkill of bologna sandwiches, hot dogs and sauce, and canned corned beef, I realized I had to improvise with ingredients that were similar to those we were accustomed to. Spinach became dasheen bush for our beloved Callaloo soup, imitation crab had to work for fresh crab and a block of coconut cream replaced freshly grated dry coconut. Over time, with the influx of immigrants from Africa, Latin America and Asia, grocers started to take our demands more

seriously. Plus, ethic type grocery stores where we could buy goods from our countries started to pop up. Times were changing!

During those years, my aunt became my sensei and much credit goes to her for the curry dishes I now prepare. Making meals in our tiny apartment kitchen was fun, especially when my cousins (her elder daughters) came over and we cooked as a family. Meanwhile, summer meant getting together for picnics, beach limes (trips to the lake) and simple backyard parties! It was then that I began to experiment with the barbecue and it became my first love for preparing meals.

I hate wasting time. So, even after moving to Canada, I was never a TV person. But after seeing my first episode of the PBS cooking show "The Urban Peasant", I was hooked on cooking programs. It was a good addiction because I would put what I saw on TV to use in the kitchen. I, however, didn't cook the recipes. Instead, I employed the preparation methods of celeb chefs to experiment with Caribbean ingredients.

When my three daughters started to eat solids, I invested even more time in the kitchen because I wanted them to appreciate, from an early age, the flavours of the Caribbean. It was always a balancing act, as I didn't want to exclude them from other types of food. As a result, our kitchen came to mimic a United Nations cafeteria. It was out of the need to document recipes for my girls that CaribbeanPot.com came into existence. Soon, what was intended to be a resource for my daughters started to attract global visitors. Now, on a monthly basis, I cook for over one million people and just a handful of them have actually tasted anything I've made.

After announcing my trip to the Caribbean online, people were excited because they knew that I would take them along on the culinary journey to my beautiful Trinidad and Tobago. It is the first time since the birth of the website that I've been able to go back with the intention of documenting the culinary culture of the islands. The past four years have only seen me do so from the confines of my humble kitchen in southern Ontario.

This book is a homecoming for many and for others it is an introduction to the rich, complex and diverse Caribbean cuisine. We'll explore flavours and ingredients that may seem new, exciting and maybe even intimidating. Fear not! I will hold your hand and guide you as if you were in my kitchen and we were preparing a meal together.

As the plane cruises towards Trinidad, I am no longer that little boy who fell in love with food at such a young age. I am a big man (maybe that explains why these seats are so uncomfortable), living in a massive country, far away from the Caribbean. But I know home will always be those two little islands where it all started. ◗

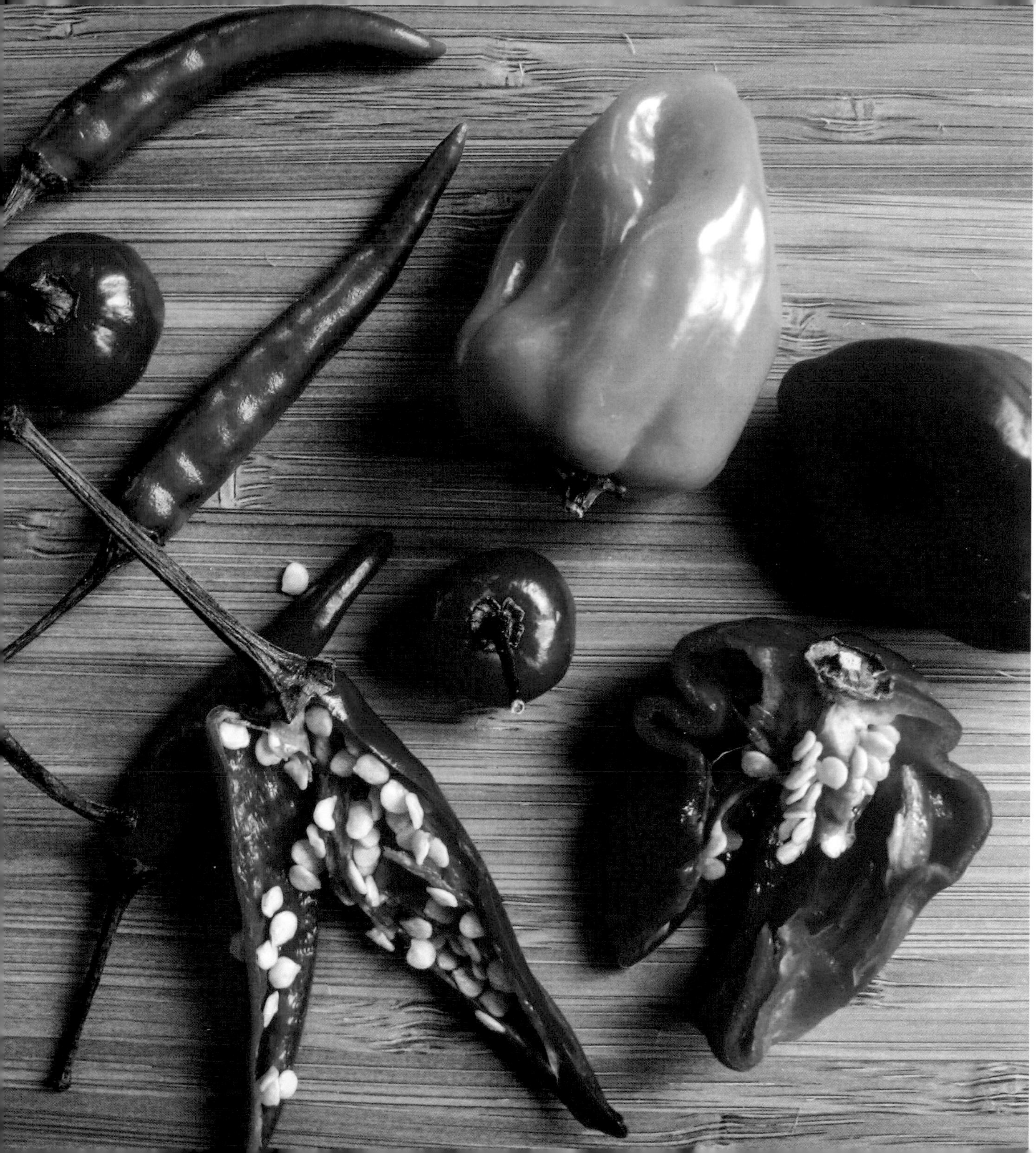

It may shock you to learn that I have not eaten a banana in the past twenty years and I only started eating mangoes again about four years ago. As a kid on the islands, I had several bananas patches (a collection of banana trees) in my backyard, so they were a daily snack. So much so that they're no longer appealing to me, especially with the comparatively bland flavour of the imported bananas in North America. Aside from my banana bingeing, I existed for mango season. In the countryside, mangoes of all shapes, sizes and flavours surrounded me. I loved them so much that I recall being sick from eating too many as a young fella.

Needless to say, in the Caribbean we have a natural abundance of tropical fruit. Yet it's not uncommon to find fruit from more temperate climates—apples, pears, grapes and strawberries—on sale. The sad part is that due to this importation of foreign fruit, many of today's youth are unfamiliar with many of the indigenous ones.

If I were to go in-depth about the fruit we're blessed with on the islands, it would be enough content to fill a book. So, I'll concentrate on four fruits you may have skipped by in the grocery store because you don't know much about them.

Dragon Fruit

Dragon fruit is most often chilled and cut in half so the flesh may be spooned out. The interior is white with edible black seeds and has a sort of firm but creamy texture. Its juice is also used in frozen drinks. When shopping for dragon fruit, you'll notice that they are usually individually wrapped and in some cases have a padding to protect them during shipping. Look for ones that are bright in colour and have no blemishes. Also, check the bottom stem to make sure the dragon fruit is not starting to rot.

The red fruit (there are also pink and yellow variations) is high in lycopene, which is a natural antioxidant that is known to prevent cancer.

Star Fruit (Carambola, Five-finger)

Star fruit is a lovely fruit that is eaten fresh, and used as a garnish in salads and drinks. When shopping for star fruit, you're looking for ones that are brilliant yellow in colour, and have no blemishes or bruises. If you see that some of the edges are going brown, the star fruit is past its prime. Also, avoid those that are greenish.

To enjoy star fruit, wash, pat dry and slice. The shape will add some contrast to your fruit salad. But to be quite honest, star fruit can be a bit bland in taste.

Papaya (Papaw or Pawpaw on the islands)

Ripe papayas take on a lovely yellow-orange colour and it's not uncommon to see dark spots as they overripen. When shopping for papaya, look for ones that are firm, have no blemishes or dark spots and boast skin with a sort of shiny gloss. If you hold one up to your nose, there should be a lovely fruity scent.

When working with green papaya for salads, you can use the steps on the next page to prepare it. However, I would recommend wearing gloves or coating your hands with a little bit of vegetable oil, as the green papaya has a sort of sticky whitish sap that can stain your hands.

EASY-PEASY PINEAPPLE PREP

1 Lay the pineapple on its side, trim off about 1/4 inch from the top and bottom and discard.

2 Stand the pineapple up on a flat work surface and with a sharp, serrated knife use a sawing motion to remove the skin from top to bottom. Go deep enough to remove any indentations.

3 With the skin removed, cut the peeled pineapple in half. Lay the two halves flat side down to make further cutting easier. Cut each half into three or four pieces lengthwise.

4 You now have long wedges (spears) of peeled pineapple. There is a core on what used to be the inside of the pineapple that is about 1/2 inch thick. Trim this off and discard.

5 Rinse with cool water. You now have peeled and cored pineapple spears to cut into pieces for use. Enjoy!

Pineapple

Along with mangoes, pineapples are among the most widely used tropical fruit in the world and can be easily found in supermarkets. Ripe pineapples will be yellow on the outside with green accents and have a wonderful scent. If you purchase one that is dark green on the outside, leave it on your kitchen counter for a few days and it will ripen naturally. Your entire kitchen will have a wonderful fruity aroma. But be warned, it does attract fruit flies during hot summer days.

Sadly, most people don't know how to peel and core pineapples so they go for the canned version. There's no reason why you should not be serving your family freshly sliced pineapple. At the time of writing, I paid $1.75 for a massive fresh pineapple, which was twenty-five cents more than a small can of diced pineapple.

Four Steps to Papaya

1 Cut the papaya lengthwise, so you have two halves and the black seeds, which look like peppercorns, are exposed.

2 Using a spoon, scoop out the seeds and discard.

3 Using a sharp paring knife, remove the outer skin and discard.

4 Rinse with cool water and cut into chunks. Enjoy!

Bitter Melon's Makeover

Bitter melon goes by a few names. Scientifically, it is called Momordica charantia. In the Caribbean, it is known as caraili. Meanwhile, other places around the world refer to it as bitter gourd or bitter squash. Bitter melon originated in the Indian subcontinent and probably made its way to the Caribbean via the indentured labourers, who came to work the sugarcane fields after slavery was abolished and there was a labour shortage in the once-lucrative sugar industry.

Bitter melon is a fruit my mom tried, in vain, to get me and my siblings to eat because she was well aware of the health benefits. Although poor mom attempted to make this extremely bitter fruit more appetizing in a few ways, nothing worked. Today, there's the odd time I will eat it—but only after following the tip mom revealed for removing most of the bitter taste. The other rule to me eating bitter melon is that it must be cooked with crispy fried saltfish.

BYE-BYE BITTERNESS

❶ Wash the melon and pat it dry with paper towels.

❷ Cut it into two pieces then lengthwise (only the thickness of the skin). You should have two cylindrical pieces of bitter melon. This will allow you to remove, with a small spoon, the innards, which you will discard.

❸ Slice it thinly so you have wheel shapes. Sprinkle salt all over the sliced bitter melon and toss it well. Let that sit for at least one hour.

❹ Using your hands or a tea towel, give the salted and sliced bitter melon a good squeeze to remove all the liquid. The salt will have drawn out most of the moisture from the bitter melon and in doing so, removed the bitterness.

❺ Rinse with cool water and squeeze again. This will help to remove any remaining bitterness and salt. Cook as you normally would.

Medicinal Melon: Bitter melon has been used in traditional medicine for several ailments, including dysentery, colic, fevers, burns, painful menstruation, scabies and other skin problems. It has also been used as abortifacient for birth control and to help in childbirth.

People throughout the Caribbean have a love affair with plantains. They are used in one form or another (boiled, fried, grilled, steamed and added to soups) by the Spanish, French and English-speaking islands. When I visited Cuba, I dined in a Havana restaurant and saw green plantains treated as we would potatoes. In Puerto Rico, I enjoyed Mofongo and Tostones—mashed, twice-fried plantain with other ingredients. In Haiti, you'd have deep fried green plantains served with Griot (fried pork) and Sauce Ti Malice. Meanwhile, Jamaicans fry sweet plantains as an accompaniment to jerk meats since the sweetness helps to balance the seasoning's spicy flavours. Other than my mom simply boiling plantains as part of her Sunday spread, I've always enjoyed sliced, ripe plantains that have been sprinkled with brown sugar and cinnamon then baked in the oven (see CaribbeanPot.com for the recipe).

Plantains are very similar to bananas but are larger in size, and contain more starch and less sugar. They are, therefore, cooked before being eaten. Green plantains are firm and starchy, and resemble potatoes in flavour. When shopping for plantains, you may see them being sold "green" and that is quite normal as there are recipes that call for them in this form. Yellow plantains are softer and starchy, but sweet. Extremely ripe plantains have a softer, deep yellow

pulp that is much sweeter than the earlier stages of ripeness. It's also not strange to see plantains being sold with dark or black spots—they may even look rotten if you don't know better.

FRIED PLANTAIN: A CLASSIC SIDE DISH

❶ Purchase the green or half-ripe (pale yellow skin) plantain. Place it in a warm,

dark corner of your kitchen for a few days. It will go from pale yellow to a darker yellow and finally start taking on dark spots. The darker the skin gets (but still firm to touch), the sweeter the plantain will be.

❷ Peel, slice and fry the plantain in vegetable oil.

Safety First: When handling green plantains (especially if they are fresh off the tree), wear gloves or coat your hands with vegetable oil. The sticky sap can cause irritation and discolour your hands. Also, don't let the sap get in contact with your eyes or clothing.

In the Caribbean, okra—or ochro as it's commonly known—is an abundantly available plant. But when people think of okra, they associate it with being slimy and this texture can be a turn-off. I personally don't mind the sliminess in soups, stews and when okra is steamed with fish. But when it is pan-fried with shrimp and/or saltfish, I much prefer okra to be as dry as possible.

MY MOM'S SAY BYE TO OKRA SLIME TECHNIQUE

1 Wash and pat okra dry with paper towels. Ensure it dries well.

2 Cut the okra into wheels or any shape you like, remembering to trim off and discard the stems.

3 Arrange it in a single layer on a paper towel or tea towel-covered cookie sheet and place it out in the sun for a couple of hours. If you happen to be dealing with winter conditions, leave the okra in a dry corner of your kitchen for a couple of hours. The air or sun will dry off most of the okra's moisture and prevent it from going slimy.

Ground provisions or "food", as they're commonly known in Jamaica, are the variety of vegetable staples cultivated and used in the Caribbean as other cultures would use potatoes. Yams, dasheen, eddoes (coco), sweet potato, cassava (yuca), green cooking banana (green fig), breadfruit, plantain and tania all fall under the "food" umbrella. Whether boiled, fried, roasted or in soups and stews, ground provisions are an important element of a Caribbean diet.

For the most part, these items are very starchy and those such as yams, eddoes and dasheen may leave a slimy texture on your hands, which can cause irritation and itchiness. When peeling or handling ground provisions, it's best to wear gloves or at least coat your hands with a little vegetable oil to form a sort of protective layer.

The green cooking banana is unlike the ripe bananas you'd typically purchase. It is actually especially grown to be cooked (boiled in most cases). It also releases a sap that can stain and cause your hands to itch so, again, coat your hands with vegetable oil when handling it. Lastly, be sure to keep the sap away from your clothing or risk them getting ruined.

When shopping for ground provisions, treat them as you would any other vegetables and look for blemishes. Make sure they are firm and have a good overall appearance. If they still intimidate you, simply ask your grocer for assistance.

Jamaican callaloo and saltfish

soup-like dish that is usually served with Macaroni Pie, stewed meats, rice, fried plantains and some sort of side salad. The base for this meal is the tender baby leaves of the dasheen (taro) plants, which are combined with diced pumpkin, onion, garlic, scotch bonnet pepper, coconut milk, thyme, okra, green onions (known as chives and pronounced "sives") and pimento peppers. Traditionally, ocean crabs are used to add another layer of flavour, so alternatively the dish is called Crab and Callaloo. There are also variations in which salted pigtails or salted beef are used instead of or in conjunction with crabs to flavour the completed product. Everything is slow cooked then whisked to a smooth consistency, which is quite filling on its own.

So what did we learn about callaloo, kids? Essentially, in Jamaica it's the amaranth plant and in other parts of the Caribbean it's a combination of ingredients that makes up a lovely soup-like dish.

Throughout my years as a food blogger and recipe video producer, I've seen many battles—predominately between Trinbagonians (people from Trinidad and Tobago) and Jamaicans—over callaloo. Both sides are very passionate about what they refer to as callaloo, as both callaloos can be identified as national dishes. Let me put this debate to rest once and for all.

When my Jamaican brothers and sisters refer to callaloo, they are referencing an actual plant called amaranth. A leafy green vegetable, it is commonly cooked with saltfish and other flavour ingredients like garlic, onion, scotch bonnet peppers and thyme. Jamaican callaloo is usually served with fried dumplings, boiled green bananas, yams and sweet potatoes.

The Jamaican version of the amaranth plant is specifically grown to be eaten as a leafy green, so the leaves are much bigger than those of the plant when it is found growing in the wild. Even the stems

Trini Callaloo

Amaranth

are very tender, although you'd think they would be tough because of their thickness. Amaranth's flavour is very similar to spinach, Swiss chard and collard greens, but it may have a slight bitter undertone that is mellowed by the other ingredients with which it's cooked.

Meanwhile, in Trinidad and Tobago (as well as Barbados, St. Lucia, Antigua, Grenada and St. Vincent), Callaloo is a rich, thick

When In Trinidad: In Trinidad and Tobago, the amaranth plant is known as spinach or chorai bhaji and can be found growing wild, especially when the first rains of rainy season arrive.

② You should now have two pieces of coconut still in the shell. Tap on each piece and then, using a butter knife, pry the coconut flesh away from the shell.

③ Wash the pieces of coconut flesh and chop them into smaller pieces to lessen the work for your food processor or blender.

④ Place the chopped coconut flesh and two cups of water into the food processor or blender and puree until you have a shredded, soggy consistency.

⑤ Strain the liquid into a bowl and squeeze out any remaining liquid from the shredded coconut. Instead of just using your hands, place the shredded coconut into a tea towel or cheesecloth. This allows you to squeeze out more liquid. What you end up with is pure coconut milk.

Coconut milk is the not-so-secret ingredient in Grenadian Oil Down, Trinbagonian Pelau, and Jamaican Rice and Peas. Although it adds an exquisite richness to any dish, like many cooks, I'm guilty of using coconut milk from a can. The thing about coconut milk is it's so easy to prepare at home that you should be making it instead of buying the canned stuff. And with the accessibility of power appliances like blenders and food processors, we don't have to toil with the grater—as our parents did—to make coconut milk. I still remember trying to help my mom and grating part of my fingers. That was the first and last time I ever grated coconut.

MADE FRESH

① Hold the coconut in one hand over the sink. Use the back ridge of a Chinese cleaver, large chef's knife or a hammer and firmly tap it in the centre. You may have to hit it a few times before it cracks and the water pours out. It is very important not to use the sharp side of the knife or cleaver.

Shake It Like A Salt Shaker: Make sure you shake the coconut before you purchase it to ensure you can hear the sound of liquid swishing around inside. If there's no liquid, don't leave the supermarket with it.

I remember the first time I watched the Food Network. I don't recall the show or the host but it was time to season the chicken when I tuned in. The "seasoning" was just salt and black pepper sprinkled onto the chicken breast. Huh? When someone from the Caribbean mentions seasoning meats and fish, rest assured they're being *seasoned*! In addition to salt and pepper, a heaping teaspoon of green seasoning and other flavour enhancers are always added. Only then does the marinating start and usually lasts overnight or at least a couple of hours.

Having said that, there is one must-have ingredient in the Caribbean Kitchen: the versatile green seasoning—a pureed mixture of fresh herbs, peppers, citrus juices or vinegar, olive oil and, at times, even spices. Even though my family had a kitchen garden with various fresh herbs, my mom always kept a container with her personalized green seasoning in the fridge.

Never buy the bottled stuff you see in the supermarkets. There's a lot of filler, colouring, preservatives and salt in the pre-packaged brands, and making the "real" thing is very simple.

GO GREEN AT HOME

Green seasoning is something you will quickly learn to personalize to your own taste by employing ingredients you appreciate. Here is a guide to get you started:

- Wiri wiri peppers
- Bird's eye pepper
- Garlic
- Lemon juice
- Pimento peppers
- Thyme
- Shado beni
- Scotch bonnet peppers
- Green onions
- Shallots
- Parsley
- Chinese celery
- Olive oil

Traditionally, my mom used a food mill (the same one she would employ for making pepper sauce and grinding the boiled dhal for Dhalpuri) to combine the green seasoning ingredients. Today, you can get excellent results with a food processor or blender.

You will need a liquid to puree the ingredients in the blender or food processor. You can use vinegar, but do keep in mind that the vinegar will cause the vibrant colours of the green seasoning to fade as it sits in the fridge. The strong Caribbean flavours, however, will still be very present.

I like using half a cup of good olive oil and a little lemon or lime juice. Water is always a good alternative as well. The amount of liquid you use will depend on the texture you want to achieve. I like my green seasoning a bit chunky, but I know my mom prefers hers very pureed and almost runny.

Even More Green Fun

What Goes In

- Use herbs you like and in whatever amount you prefer.

- If you can source it, Spanish thyme is a key ingredient. If not, fresh oregano is a good alternative.

- The hot peppers—bird's eye, scotch bonnet and wiri wiri—are optional.

- Try to source pimento peppers because they add a wonderful flavour.

- If you can't get shado beni, use cilantro.

- I prefer not to use onion, as I find it diminishes the shelf life of the seasoning.

- You're free to add spices to the mix as well, but it will change the overall flavour.

- Pre-chop the ingredients to make them easier to process.

Storage

Place the green seasoning in a glass or disposable plastic container in the fridge. It will last about six months. But be warned, the container will stain and take on the scent/flavour of the green seasoning. You can also freeze the green seasoning into ice cubes and then place them in a freezer lock bag. The second option is just a matter of taking out a cube when you're ready to season your favourite meat and fish. By the way, this is a good base for making meat and even vegetarian curries.

Step Up Steak

Take one tablespoon of green seasoning and add it to two tablespoons of olive oil. Drizzle onto steaks and let that marinate for about 30 minutes before grilling. The result is absolutely divine!

In the Caribbean, we're all about fresh ingredients, bold spices and fragrant herbs. One of the fondest memories I have of my childhood is the day I was assigned the task of gathering herbs for my mom so she could season the chicken for Sunday lunch. Sunday lunch is the "big meal" of the week and much emphasis is placed on making it one to remember. So, while green seasoning is the everyday go-to for flavouring and marinating meats, Sunday lunch highlights fresh ingredients. Scouting the garden for herbs for mom was a very important task and being part of this grand Sunday tradition is something I've cherished in the years since.

Fresh thyme, Spanish thyme, shado beni and ginger were usually on the list of items I had to source. These herbs would then be combined with the bunch of sives (green onions), celery and parsley mom would get from the market.

Spanish Thyme

Spanish Thyme (plectranthus amboinicus)

Spanish thyme is also known as podina, big leaf thyme, oregano de cartagena (in Cuba) and oregano brujo (in Puerto Rico).

Spanish thyme has an oregano-like flavour and odour. It is used in conjunction with other herbs to season meats and as a means of adding additional flavour to curry dishes. It can be a bit overwhelming, so it's used in moderation. Though you can now get it in dried form, fresh Spanish thyme leaves are much more preferable. Sage and/or oregano can be used as a substitute.

Shado Beni (eryngium foetidum)

Thyme (thymus vulgaris)

This is one herb that is much loved and used throughout the Caribbean. Not to mention, it was always a favourite for me to harvest during my days as mom's herb guy! After a slight bruising, you'll get a lovely aroma from the tiny leaves. These leaves can be added to marinades or directly into a pot as its contents simmer. A good Rice and Peas is not the same without fresh sprigs, to be removed after the dish is cooked.

Fresh thyme should be wrapped in a slightly damp paper towel and stored in the refrigerator. At the end of the summer growing season, I usually reap and dry as much thyme as I can for the winter months. Dried thyme can be placed in a tightly sealed glass container and stored in a cool, dark and dry place, where it will keep fresh for up to six months. It retains its flavour better than many other herbs, but I always much prefer the fresh stuff.

Did you know that thyme leaves are one of the richest sources of potassium, iron, calcium, manganese, magnesium, and selenium?

This herb is referred to as chadon, shadon, shado beni, shadow benny, bandhania and culantro. Other common names include: recao (in Puerto Rico), long coriander, wild or Mexican coriander and sawtooth coriander. If you reside in North America, you can find shado beni in Asian grocery stores where it goes by its Vietnamese name: ngò gai.

Similar in flavour and scent to cilantro (which makes a good substitute if you can't source it), shado beni is more intense. It is used primarily in the Southern Caribbean for seasoning meats and fish, and in hot sauces and chutneys. Yet another herb that can be overpowering and should be used in moderation, shado beni is great when finely chopped and used as a finish for curry dishes (and it's my mom's secret for curry fish).

Wrap shado beni in a damp paper towel and keep it in the fridge or place it, root down, into a glass with about one or two inches of water.

Chinese celery

Scallion

This is one of the most versatile herbs in a Caribbean cook's arsenal and the uses are endless. I must explain though that what we refer to as scallion in the Caribbean is a bit different than spring or green onion. Scallion has a sort of reddish bulb at the root and is much more intense in flavour than green onion. There's a sort of garlic or shallot taste to it that is not as pronounced as the flavour of onion.

Celery (Chinese celery)

Unlike North American celery (apium graveolens var. dulce), which is grown and used primarily as a vegetable, the Caribbean version is grown for the leaves, which are treated as an herb. It is used

in making green seasoning, on its own in marinades and chopped finely as a finishing topping for various dishes.

My favourite memory of celery is the day I had my great aunt Blacina's Chicken Pelau. Just before it was done cooking, she sprinkled in some finely chopped celery leaves. Wow, what a difference!

Rosemary (rosmarinus officinalis)

This is not a very popular herb in the Caribbean, as it's not native to the region. However, you'll still find it in herb boxes and it's easily accessible in grocery stores. The leaves are used as flavouring when stuffing and roasting lamb or making pork, chicken and turkey.

Basil (ocimum basilicum)

I don't ever recall seeing my mom use basil. This may be because at that time it was

foreign to us. However, it's an herb that is becoming popular as Caribbean cooks travel more and experiment with different flavours.

Basil leaves contain health benefiting essential oils such as eugenol, citronellol, linalool, citral, limonene and terpineol. These compounds are known to have anti-inflammatory and anti-bacterial properties.

Parsley (petroselinum crispum)

In most cases, it's usually the flat leaf or Italian version of the herb that we use on the islands. But for some reason (it must be the Caribbean sunshine), the flavour is stronger than in North America. So, it's used in moderation as not to overpower dishes. In all honesty, parsley is not a must-have herb like thyme and scallions.

Parsley is, however, a good source of antioxidants (especially luteolin), folic acid, vitamin C, and vitamin A. Proclaimed health benefits include anti-inflammatory properties and a boost for the immune system.

1. **Mix of red and green bird's eye** (a.k.a. bird pepper)

2. **Red bird's eye**

3. **Green bird's eye**

4. **Scotch bonnet** (congo pepper)

5. **Wiri wiri** (in Guyana) or **coffee pepper** (in Trinidad and Tobago)

6. **Pimento peppers**

No Caribbean meal is complete without spices, fresh herbs and the fieriness from the many peppers used in the various recipes. So, the answer to the heat or flavour question is both, depending on how you use these little fireballs that I lovingly refer to as "Caribbean Sunshine" in my cooking videos.

A few years ago, we rented a plot of land from the City of Hamilton and had the opportunity to plant a community garden. That summer, we had a bumper crop of scotch bonnet and its close cousin, the habanero pepper. The rich reds, oranges, greens and other colours of the fully matured "Caribbean Sunshine" mesmerized my wife, Caron, so she volunteered to help me reap them. A week later, her hands were still in pain— or rather in a constant state of heat. She had not worn gloves and though none of the peppers broke during harvesting, just the oils from the outside of the peppers were enough to see her in discomfort for days. Ouch!

While Caron's incident is a cautionary tale, don't be intimidated by it. You can easily prevent the pain and control the heat by personalizing the dishes you make.

Prevent Pain and Personalize

■ Use gloves when handling any hot peppers.

■ After handling hot peppers, immediately wash your hands with soap and water. Don't touch any part of your body until you do (I'll remind you throughout the book).

■ If you're worried about the raw heat, don't use any of the seeds or white membrane directly surrounding the seeds.

■ If you want flavour rather than raw heat, place whole hot peppers into your pot but don't break them or they will release heat. Also, remember to remove them from the pot once your dish is done.

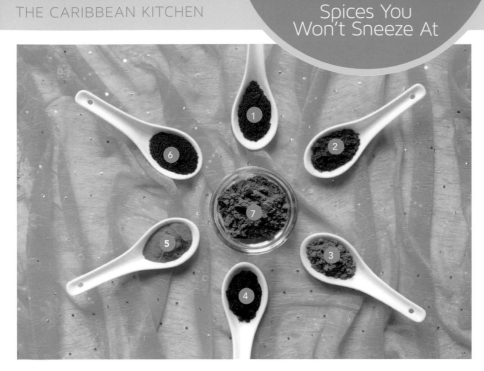

1 Roasted geera (cumin)

2 Garam masala

3 Duck/goat curry blend

4 Ground masala

5 Sorfran (tumeric)

6 Amchar masala

7 Curry powder (madras blend)

Along with a plethora of fresh produce, and quality fish and meats, Caribbean people are blessed with the knowledge of using spices to create some of the most delightful dishes on the planet. But as with most things, the way we put ingredients to use differs from island to island.

A good example is the elementary Curry Chicken—or Chicken Curry as they say

in Guyana. I've been fortunate to sample Curry Chicken from Guyana, Jamaica, St. Lucia, Antigua, Barbados, St. Thomas, Dominica and my native Trinidad and Tobago, and I can tell you that they all left a different impression on my taste buds. The colour, texture, heat and overall taste were all unique.

Because the Caribbean is a melange of African, Amerindian, British, Chinese, Dutch, French, Indian and Spanish, there's been a lot of influences on our regional cuisine—especially the spices we use. Cinnamon, nutmeg, allspice and star anise may be native (to some extent) to the Caribbean, but the Indian indenture labourers brought with them many curry and masala blends. If you really want to experience the Indian influence (spice-wise) on our cuisine, I invite you to visit Trinidad and Tobago. You'll taste some of the most unique blends when it comes to curries and masalas. Some are even designed especially for cooking certain meats like duck and goat—in which heat plays a big role.

For the most part, we use curry powders on the islands and it's uncommon to see people making their own blends or pastes. The curry powders made and sold in the Caribbean mimic the madras blends out of India. But for some reason they take on a twist when cooked, with a unique colour, scent and heat.

Along with exciting curry blends, you'll also find roasted geera (cumin), garam masala, ground masala, amchar masala and sorfran (turmeric) being used on a regular basis. I can still picture my great aunt's garden, in which she grew sorfran. A plant that is similar to ginger with the same sort of fleshy root, sorfran is harvested, dried and ground into a brilliant yellow powder to use in dhals and in any good curry blend.

Meanwhile, allspice (a.k.a. pimenta dioica), despite its name, is a single spice. Known as pimento berries, it is a key ingredient in Jamaican jerk marinades. Pimento wood also plays an important part in achieving the perfect jerk as it burns and adds a lovely flavour to the meats being cooked over it. You can get pimento berries whole or ground into a powder, which makes it very convenient to use.

Finally, what would Caribbean-style Chinese food be without five-spice powder brought over by the Chinese workers? A combination of five aromatic spices, five-spice powder is excellent when used as a marinade for chicken (see the Grilled Five-Spice Chicken recipe on page 50).

DIY Chinese Five-Spice Powder: To make quick Chinese five-spice powder, toast and grind one teaspoon each ground cinnamon, ground cloves, fennel seed, star anise and Szechwan peppercorns.

Flavour Beyond the Spices!

From the orange peel my family always had hanging in a corner of the kitchen to the mornings my mom would ask either me or my brother to get her some leaves from the soursop tree, I grew up not only with an appreciation for flavours, but also learning to use them for maximum results.

I recall, for example, how important it was for mom to have pimento peppers to add that "special" taste to her stewed meats. Not to mention, the base of all good Caribbean food—green seasoning—was not complete without these fragrant peppers. The dried orange peel, on the other hand, would be used to make a refreshing tea, flavour stews, in mauby and sorrel drinks, and to add the finishing touch to cake batter.

MUST-HAVE CARIBBEAN FLAVOURS

Ginger

It is essential in stewed meats, marinades, tea or ginger beer and a must for making delicious Jamaican jerked meats. Hints of ginger can also be found in traditional drinks like sorrel and mauby.

Dried Orange Peel

Used primarily as a flavour enhancer in brewed drinks, especially as a tea, you won't believe the difference dried orange peel makes. To make a tea, pour hot water over dried orange peel, steep, sweeten with sugar or honey and be prepared for a refreshing and calming beverage.

Lime Zest

No cake batter would be complete without this lovely touch of citrus. Lime zest also works well in marinades and some salad dressings.

Soursop Leaves

The soursop leaves are brewed like a tea and supposedly help to calm the stomach.

Fever Grass (lemon grass)

I think it's weird that the plant known as lemon grass everywhere else is referred to as fever grass in the Caribbean. Either way, it's a great addition to curries and stir-fry dishes. I also remember my dad making hot cups of tea with the root of the lemon grass whenever my siblings or I had a high temperature. And if you're wondering, yes, it did work.

Cloves

Besides being a flavour enhancer for brewed drinks, Christmas ham always benefits from the lovely aroma of cloves—as do spiced cakes.

Cinnamon Stick

It's best added to Pelau (strange but true), curries, and brewed drinks such as mauby and sorrel. And how could I not mention homemade chocolate tea (a.k.a. cocoa tea)?

Vanilla

Baking would never be the same without this wonderful extract. Also, add a drop or two of vanilla to citrus juices and you'll notice how it changes the dynamic of these beverages.

Mixed Essence

A combination vanilla, kola, almond, pear and cherry extracts, mixed essence is an absolute must in cakes. And if you think

the drop of vanilla in your citrus drinks is amazing, wait until you add some mixed essence.

Star Anise

With its lovely licorice flavour, star anise is great in brewed drinks. Personally, however, it's not a flavour I like so chances are you won't see me using this in my recipes anytime soon.

Handling Ginger: With a scraping motion, use a spoon to remove the skin off fresh ginger. This way, you have minimal wastage.

1 **Lemon grass** (a.k.a. fever grass)
2 **Cinnamon**
3 **Pimento peppers**
4 **Ginger**
5 **Nutmeg**
6 **Limes**
7 **Dried orange peel**
8 **Cloves**
9 **Bay leaves**
10 **Star anise**

If you're familiar with the curry dishes of the Caribbean, you'll notice that the cooking process is very similar whether you're currying meat, seafood or vegetables. However, you may find subtle differences from island to island. In Jamaica, for instance, when making Curry Goat, the curry goes into the marinating process and a little more is added as it cooks. Meanwhile, in Guyana, Trinidad and Tobago, and some of the other countries, the curry is toasted or fried before adding meat, vegetables or seafood to the pot.

SEASONED FIRST

Cut the meat of choice into pieces, wash it thoroughly, drain it dry and season it with the ingredients in which it will be marinating. Herbs, onions, garlic, a tomato or two, salt, black pepper, a pinch of cinnamon and curry powder is a common combination. After marinating, heat some vegetable oil on high and sear the meat. As it comes up to a boil, you'll add another dusting of curry powder and allow it to finish cooking.

HOW MOM TAUGHT US

My mom seasons the meat with all her herbs and spices, and allows it to marinate. She then heats vegetable oil in the classic dutchie (iron pot), adds chopped garlic along with onion and cooks that for a couple of minutes. As the garlic and onion cook, she adds curry powder and some water to a small bowl to form a sort of slurry. The slurry is then poured into the pot, the heat is reduced to low and the curry is allowed to cook. This awakens the spices that make up the curry and takes the rawness out of it. After the slurry has cooked down until it is grainy and the oil with which mom started is visible, she adds her seasoned meat and cooks until it is done. If she is cooking vegetables, mom adds the vegetables as she would the seasoned meat, tops with salt, black pepper, scotch bonnet, etc., and allows it to cook until the veggies are tender. For this technique, you may need to add liquid such as water or coconut milk.

MY WAY (A.K.A THE BEST WAY!)

I like to toast the curry powder before adding anything to the pot. In the case of chicken, I season it as I normally would. Then I heat vegetable oil in a deep, heavy pot, add some diced garlic, onion and ginger (if I'm looking for something different), and cook it on low heat. After three to four minutes, with my heat as low as it can go, in goes the Caribbean-style madras blend curry powder. I stir to let it toast and get up close and personal with the garlic and onion. The toasting releases a wealth of flavour and you're on your way to a good curry. Next, I add half a cup of water, bring it to a boil and allow it simmer for a few minutes. After toasting the curry, this step cooks the rawness out of it. Once it's simmered for a bit, I turn up the heat to burn off all the liquid and intensify the curry flavour before adding seasoned meats or vegetables. Be sure to burn off the liquid until you have a dark grainy texture before adding whatever you're currying.

A Dash of Something Extra: Add some cinnamon to your curry dishes for a unique twist on things.

The One That Didn't Get Away

Grilled, stewed, curried, fried, steamed and even raw—as was the case with the oyster cocktails I enjoyed as a boy in the south Trinidad town of Marabella—I love seafood. And the concoction of herbs, lime juice, hot sauces and freshly shucked oysters still leaves me yearning for those days in Marabella.

Islanders, in general, have a natural affinity for fish and seafood. That's probably because most of the islands that make up the Caribbean are so small that getting fresh catch of the day, even in the interior, is not uncommon. I remember fish being relatively inexpensive as there weren't any processing plants, so the fishermen had to sell their catch within hours of offloading it from their boats. I was always mesmerized by how sharp the fishmongers' knives were, and how

effortlessly and gracefully they used them to clean the fish. It was as if these fishmongers had a sort of inner rhythm they were following to scale, gut and trim the fins.

It still amazes me how many people love fish but are so turned off by its appearance that they won't cook it. We must, however, employ our senses when shopping for fish, so be prepared to get up close and personal. Start off by looking at the eyes. They should be bright and clear. Fish with dull or cloudy eyes may be safe to eat, but they are not fresh. Next, look at the body of the fish. It should have a natural shine that is almost metallic in appearance. If it looks dull or has discoloured patches, the fish is past its prime and I would avoid buying it. Smell it—a fresh fish should smell

like the ocean or clean water. Under no circumstances should you buy a "fishy smelling" fish. Cooking won't improve it. The gills also have a story to tell. They should be a rich red. If the fish is old, the gills will turn the colour of faded brick and the edges will take on a sort of brownish tint. Lastly, if you're able to, press the skin with your finger. It should be resilient enough so your indentation disappears. If your fingerprint remains, move on.

Fillet-o-Shine: If you are shopping for fish fillets, look for vibrant flesh. Fish fades as it ages. If the fillet still has skin, that skin should look as pristine as it would were the fish whole. It should also still have that natural shine.

OUT WITH THE SALT

1 Place the saltfish in a deep bowl and cover it with cool water. Allow it to soak overnight for best results.

2 Drain and place the fish in a deep pot then cover it with water and, on high heat, bring it to a boil. As it comes to a boil, reduce to a rolling boil and allow it to boil for about 25 minutes.

3 Drain, rinse with cool water and allow the fish to cool completely before handling it.

4 Squeeze out as much of the water as you can then flake the fish with two forks, use your hands to break it up or pound it into the texture for which your recipe calls.

My mom would send my siblings and I "up the road" (street) to the village "shop" (store) whenever she ran out of saltfish—especially if the meal she was preparing depended heavily on the unique flavour only this key ingredient offers. The "shop" doubled as the village bar, pool hall and grocery. On the weekends you could even purchase cooked foods like Souse, Blood Pudding and Pholourie. There was always a buzz of activity, so my brother and I were never as direct as our mom would want us to be. Yet, mom always made a point of saying to come home immediately after we made the purchase: "One pong (pound) of saltfish and come straight home."

Saltfish, as it's lovingly known in the Caribbean, plays a huge part in our culinary culture. That's why you'll find it used in countless ways as you make your way up and down the island chain. Originally, cod was the fish of choice for dried and salted preservation purposes, so it's not strange that "salted cod" became a sort of generic name for saltfish in the region. With cod stocks at an all-time low, other varieties of white fish are now used to make saltfish. These include pollock, haddock, blue whiting, ling and tusk.

One of the common questions I get from foodies who are not familiar with saltfish is, "Chris, why do you remove the salt from the fish? Why not just use fresh unsalted fish?" The method of salting and drying the fish means the level of salt makes the fish unusable directly. But once prepared in the following simple steps, the overall flavour it will add to your dishes is amazing. That's because this process removes the raw salty taste the saltfish would have and in the process re-hydrates it a bit from its dried state. You're then set to add a wonderful layer of flavour to many Caribbean dishes.

Hold The Salt: Even though you soaked, boiled and rinsed it, the saltfish will still have some salt in it. Be sure to consider this before adding salt to any dish in which you'll be using saltfish.

Caramelized Chicken!
Won't It Be Sweet?

I've always had a weakness for stewed chicken—not to be confused with North American type stews or Jamaican Brown Stew Chicken. Variations of the stewed chicken I'm referring to can be found throughout the southern Caribbean and the French-speaking islands.

Poultry or meat is marinated overnight in wonderful green seasoning, freshly grated ginger and other flavour enhancers. Oil is heated and brown sugar is caramelized just until it starts "burning". The seasoned chicken (or pork, beef or goat) is then quickly added to the pot. The resulting dish is my absolute favourite way to enjoy chicken and is on my Top 3 Caribbean Dishes list.

STEW IT UP!

❶ Cut your meat of choice into serving sized portions, season according to the recipe you are following.

❷ Heat vegetable oil (or any oil that can withstand heat) on high.

❸ In a heavy pot, using a long-handled spoon, add brown sugar to the pot and stir it around. It will start to melt and bubble.

❹ Keep moving around the frothy-looking sugar. It will start to go darker (amber) in colour and smoke will start to develop.

❺ Make sure you have the seasoned meat very close by because you'll have to move quickly. Into your dark amber sugar-oil mix, start adding the seasoned meat. Move it around so all the pieces get coated in the

lovely caramel colour you created.

❻ Reduce the heat, cover your pot with a lid and allow the chicken to simmer for about 10 minutes. Then, uncover your pot and turn the heat back to high to burn off all the liquid. This will help to add a rich colour to the meat and infuse it with all the wonderful flavours. After you've burnt off all the liquid, the pieces of meat will have colour but still be raw and/or tough. Add water, bring it to a boil and allow the dish to simmer until the meat is fully cooked. For chicken, I would add about 3/4-cup water. For meats like pork and beef, I would add two cups of water and simmer for at least one hour so the meat is tender when done. Remember to burn off excess liquid to thicken the gravy to your likeness.

So, will it be sweet? Nope! That's because when you season the meat, you should be using chopped onion and tomato, a bit of scotch bonnet pepper and salt. This combination, along the green seasoning in which you marinated the meat, will help to nicely balance flavours.

Lime, Lemon or Vinegar!

In my younger days, I loved lime juice. Give me the juice of five limes, water, sugar to sweeten, a few drops of mixed essence and crushed ice, and I would be in heaven on those hot days. My love for limes was so real that it always got me in trouble for using the limes my mom had set aside for washing meats. No limes for mom's meats meant having to go up the road to my grandmother's and begging her for a rough skin lemon.

That woman treated her lemon tree like gold. She wouldn't even allow me to use the bamboo rod to harvest the lemon. According to her, I was hitting her precious tree and not just the lemon stem.

Over the years, I've received several e-mails asking why in the Caribbean we wash our meats and fish with lime or lemon juice (or in some cases, vinegar). I believe we grew up thinking that the acid

in these liquids helps to kill any bacteria. There could be some truth to that, as I don't remember hearing of anyone being sick from salmonella poisoning. Additionally, the lovely citrus scent is very welcoming. Cooking in the Caribbean is all about the senses, so we don't like meats having any sort of "meat" smell, referred to as "fresh" (which is similar to North Americans saying "fishy").

RUB-A-DUB-DUB

❶ Cut the chicken (for example) into serving size pieces, and, unless a recipe states otherwise, remove the skin and fat.

❷ Place the pieces of trimmed chicken into a bowl and pour in the juice of limes or lemons.

❸ Mix well and let it sit for 3-5 minutes.

❹ Add cool water and individually wash each piece. Drain, rinse with cool water and drain well again.

❺ Season as the recipe you're using indicates.

The Skinny On Skin: If you're making a dish in which the skin may be used to prevent the chicken from drying out (such as fried or barbecue chicken), skip the step in which you would remove it.

Wash That Rice Right

Forget the instant stuff that famous "uncle" sells. In the Caribbean, it's all about brown (parboiled) and white rice.

Don't get me wrong, you can get Basmati, Arborio, Jasmine and wild rice, to name a few. But the rice of choice due to availability and price is brown and white.

The thing about these two varieties of rice is that they're usually packed with grit and excess starch from the milling and polishing processes.

If cooked unwashed, you can end up with thick, soggy rice. So, it is common practice in the Caribbean to wash rice thoroughly before cooking it.

THE EASY WAY

Place the measured rice you'll be cooking in a strainer and run water straight from the tap over it. Gently massage the rice

so the running water washes away the grit and excess starch.

THE OLD SCHOOL WAY

This is the way my mom taught me. Place the measured rice in a deep bowl and cover it with water. Using your hands, massage the rice grains in a rubbing motion. The water will quickly become cloudy. Drain it and repeat the process until the water runs clear, which can take up to four times. I think "The Easy Way" is faster.

Weight Conversions

Customary quantity	Metric equivalent
1 ounce	28 g
4 ounces or 1/4 pound	113 g
1/3 pound	150 g
8 ounces or 1/2	230 g
2/3 pound	300 g
12 ounces or 3/4 pound	340 g
1 pound or 16 ounces	450 g
2 pounds	900 g

Oven Temperatures

Description	American Standard	Metric	Gas mark
very cool	225 F	110 C	mark # 1/4
luke warm	250 F	130 C	mark # 1/2
cool	275 F	140 C	mark # 1
cool moderate	300 F	150 C	mark # 2
very moderate	325 F	170 C	mark # 3
moderate	350 F	180 C	mark # 4
moderately hot	375 F	190 C	mark # 5
fairly hot	400 F	200 C	mark # 6
hot	425 F	220 C	mark # 7
really hot	450 F	230 C	mark # 8
very hot	475 F	240 C	mark # 9

Volume Conversions: Normally used for liquids only

Customary quantity	Metric equivalent
1 teaspoon	5 ml
1 tablespoon or 1/2 fluid ounce	15 ml
1 fluid ounce or 1/8 cup	30 ml
1/4 cup or 2 fluid ounces	60 ml
1/3 cup	80 ml
1/2 cup or 4 fluid ounces	120 ml
2/3 cup	160 ml
3/4 cup or 6 fluid ounces	180 ml
1 cup or 8 fluid ounces or half pint	240 ml
1 1/2 cups or 12 fluid ounces	350 ml
2 cups or 1 pint or 16 fluid ounces	475 ml
3 cups or 1 1/2 pints	700 ml
4 cups or 2 pints or 1 quart	950 ml
4 quarts or 1 gallon	3.8 L

Weights of common ingredients in grams

Ingredient	1 cup	3/4 cup	2/3 cup	1/2 cup	1/3 cup	1/4 cup	2 Tbsp
Flour, all purpose (wheat)	120 g	90 g	80 g	60 g	40 g	30 g	15 g
Flour, well sifted all purpose (wheat)	110 g	80 g	70 g	55 g	35 g	27 g	13 g
Sugar, granulated cane	200 g	150 g	130 g	100 g	65 g	50 g	25 g
Confectioner's sugar (cane)	100 g	75 g	70 g	50 g	35 g	25 g	13 g
Brown sugar, packed firmly (but not too firmly)	180 g	135 g	120 g	90 g	60 g	45 g	23 g
Corn meal	160 g	120 g	100 g	80 g	50 g	40 g	20 g
Corn starch	120 g	90 g	80 g	60 g	40 g	30 g	15 g
Rice, uncooked	190 g	140 g	125 g	95 g	65 g	48 g	24 g
Macaroni, uncooked	140 g	100 g	90 g	70 g	45 g	35 g	17 g
Couscous, uncooked	180 g	135 g	120 g	90 g	60 g	45 g	22 g
Oats, uncooked quick	90 g	65 g	60 g	45 g	30 g	22 g	11 g
Table salt	300 g	230 g	200 g	150 g	100 g	75 g	40 g
Butter	240 g	180 g	160 g	120 g	80 g	60 g	30 g
Vegetable shortening	190 g	140 g	125 g	95 g	65 g	48 g	24 g
Chopped fruits and vegetables	150 g	110 g	100 g	75 g	50 g	40 g	20 g
Nuts, chopped	120 g	90 g	80 g	60 g	40 g	30 g	15 g
Nuts, ground	60 g	45 g	40 g	30 g	20 g	15 g	8 g
Bread crumbs, dry	150 g	110 g	100 g	75 g	50 g	40 g	20 g
Parmesan cheese, grated	90 g	65 g	60 g	45 g	30 g	22 g	11 g

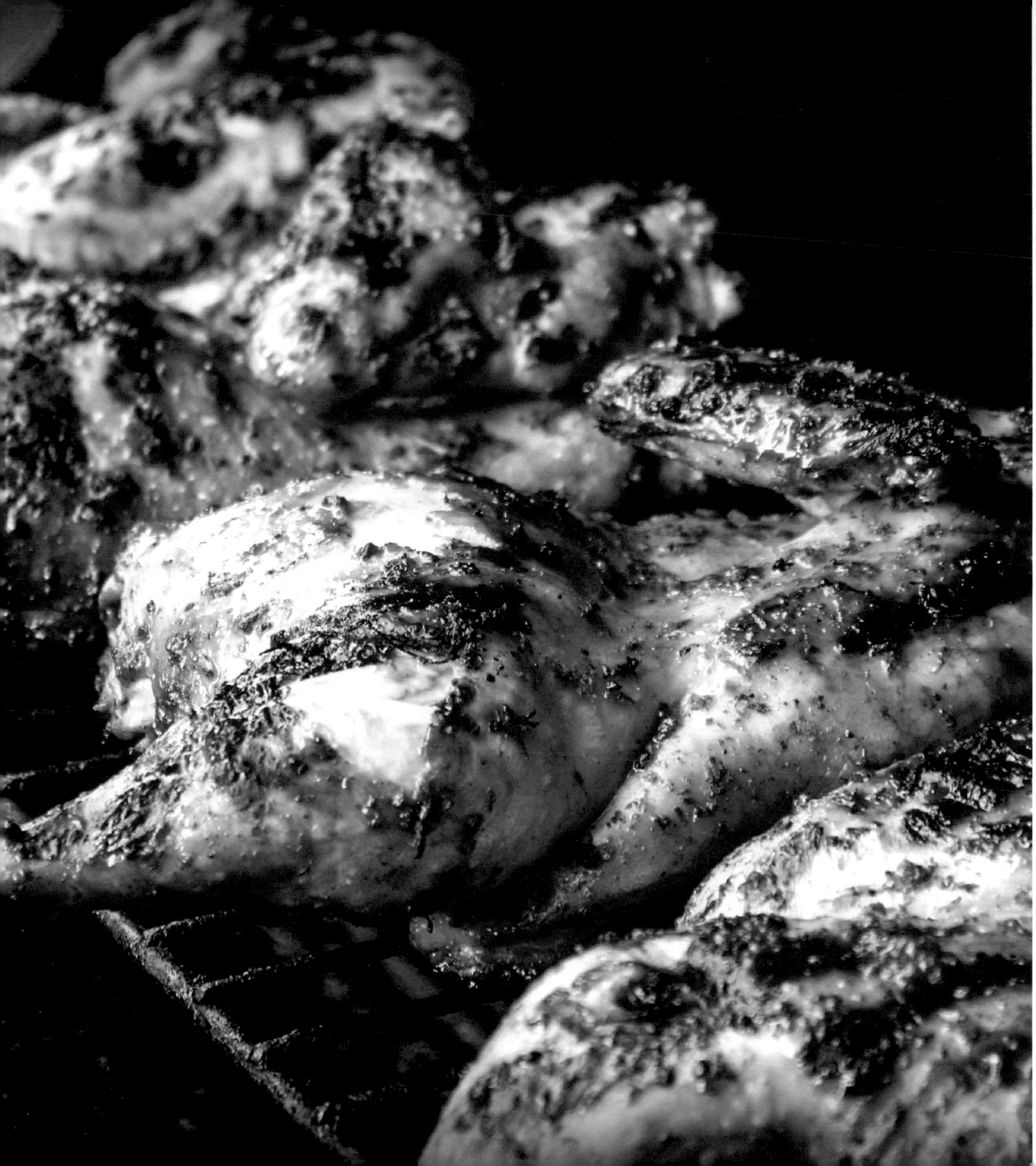

No matter how tough times were, mom always found a way to have pork, beef or chicken make its way onto the table for the traditional Caribbean Sunday lunch. Looking back, I still don't know how she made both lunch and dinner from a six-pound chicken for a family of five–and still had leftovers to add to dad's lunch the next day."

It was the norm that for our trips to the beach or for any family outing, mom would cook up a pot of Pelau to take for lunch. Nothing beat taking a swim in the ocean and making your "hungry way" back to the trunk of the car. Mom would be waiting there, ready to serve plates of still-hot Pelau with a fresh green salad on the side.

Stew chicken according to steps 1-5 in the "Caramelized Chicken! Won't It Be Sweet?" section of the book. Cover pot, reduce the heat to medium-low and cook for 10 minutes.

Meanwhile, rinse the peas in running water to get rid of the additional sodium that coats canned foods. Wash, peel and slice the carrots into coins. Remove pot lid and turn up heat to burn off all liquid in the pot then add the peas and carrots.

Replace the lid and turn down the heat as you wash the rice according to directions in the "Wash That Rice Right" section of the book.

Add rice, then the coconut milk and water, to the pot. Stir everything and bring back to a boil. Cover the pot and allow to simmer for about 35 minutes or until all the liquid is gone, and the grains of rice are tender and plump. For an additional layer of flavour, add a teaspoon of Caribbean salted butter as you turn off the stove. Stir and cover the pot for about 5 minutes.

You'll Need...

- 4-5 lbs chicken, cut into pieces
- Juice of 2 limes (to clean chicken)
- 1 tablespoon salt
- 1 teaspoon Worcestershire sauce
- 1 tablespoon ketchup
- 2 cloves garlic, crushed
- 1 teaspoon ginger, freshly grated
- 1 each medium onion and tomato, chopped
- 2-3 tablespoons cilantro
- 1/2 teaspoon black pepper
- 1/4 scotch bonnet pepper
- 1 scallion, chopped

- 2 sprigs thyme
- 2 tablespoons vegetable oil
- 2 tablespoons brown sugar
- 1 can pigeon peas
- 1 large carrot
- 3 cups long-grain brown rice
- 1 cup coconut milk
- 3 cups water
- 1 teaspoon Caribbean salted butter

Clean chicken according to the directions in the "Lime, Lemon or Vinegar!" section of the book. Season with all ingredients except oil, sugar, pigeon peas, carrot, rice, coconut milk, water and butter. Marinate for at least 1 hour.

Authenticity: Caribbean salted butter (a.k.a. Golden Ray brand) is uniquely different than traditional butter. It has a wonderful Creole flavour, which adds a distinct twist to the finished product. This butter can be found at West Indian and some Asian supermarkets.

A Dash of Something Extra: My great aunt would get a branch of celery, fresh from her garden, finely chop only the leafy part and top her Pelau with it. Stunning is the only word I can use to describe this added zing.

Ultimate Curry Chicken

Yes, I said "ultimate"! I've added my personal touch to my mom's recipe and I must say that it absolutely rocks. By toasting the curry rather than creating a slurry, as is traditionally done on the islands, this Ultimate Curry Chicken gets a wonderful overall flavour.

You'll Need...

- 3 lbs chicken
- Juice of 1 lemon (to clean chicken)
- 3/4 tablespoon salt
- Dash black pepper
- 1 medium tomato, diced
- 1 teaspoon green seasoning
- 1 scallion, chopped
- 3 tablespoons vegetable oil
- 1 medium onion, sliced
- 2 cloves garlic, sliced
- 1/4 scotch bonnet pepper (or habanero)
- 1 tablespoon shado beni
- 1 heaping tablespoon curry powder
- 1/4 teaspoon roasted cumin powder
- 6 tablespoons water
- 1 1/2 cups water

Cut the chicken into serving-sized pieces then clean according to the directions in the "Lime, Lemon or Vinegar!" section of the book. Squeeze out the chicken as best you can and place in a bowl.

Add the salt, black pepper, tomato, green seasoning and scallion to the chicken, and stir so everything gets coated. Cover bowl, place in fridge and marinate for a couple of hours.

Once it's been marinated, in a fairly large pan, heat 2 of the 3 tablespoons of oil on medium heat. Add the sliced onion, garlic and hot pepper. Allow this to cook for a few minutes until the onion goes soft and starts to turn a little bit brown. Turn the heat to low and add the shado beni to the pot, followed by the curry powder and cumin, and stir. You may notice that the pot is "dry", so add the last tablespoon of oil to ensure that nothing sticks. Follow it with 6 tablespoons of water and allow this to

cook for a couple minutes. It will bring out the true aroma of the curry.

As the liquid burns off, turn the heat back up to high and add the chicken, stirring in between each piece to ensure it gets coated in the curry. After you've added all the seasoned chicken, turn the heat to medium-low and cover the pot for 10 minutes. The chicken will spring its own juices, so after 10 minutes remove the lid and turn the heat up to high again. Burn off the liquid to infuse the chicken with the curry base. Keep stirring as the liquid burns off until you see nothing but a bit of oil with a sort of curry paste (this is the good stuff) at the bottom of the pot.

Add the 1 1/2 cups of water and bring to a boil then, with the pot covered, lower the heat to a gentle simmer. Stir occasionally and after 20 minutes, remove the lid to check if the sauce is the consistency you like. Usually, I have to turn the heat up a bit to reduce the curry because I like it a little thicker.

Choose Your Meat: I usually use dark meat (with bones) when cooking curry, as I find that the overall flavour of the finished dish is tastier. The recipe works just as well with white meat, although be warned that it is less moist.

Authenticity: Your local West Indian, Latino or Asian grocery will have shado beni. But if you don't have it or can't find it, use cilantro. That goes for all recipes in this book.

Curry-Stew Chicken Wings

Kieana, my eldest daughter, is hooked on anything stewed with brown sugar. Indy, my youngest, will not touch the stuff. She's more into curry dishes. And Kieana will only tolerate curry—no real love there. To ensure they both eat, I make a dish that was a hit when my mom would make it for my siblings and I. Curry-Stew Chicken is a combination of both curry and stewing, as the name suggests.

If you're curious, Tehya, my middle girl, is like her pops and will eat anything in sight!

Cut and trim your chicken wings, and clean them according to the directions in the "Lime, Lemon or Vinegar!" section of the book. Place the cleaned wings in a large bowl and season with all the ingredients except vegetable oil, brown sugar and water. Mix well, cover and place in the fridge to marinate for at least 2 hours.

Remove the seasoned chicken from the fridge about 15 minutes before you're ready to cook to bring it back to room temperature.

Not discarding the marinade bowl yet, stew according to steps 1-5 in the "Caramelized Chicken! Won't It Be Sweet?" section of the book. Cover the pot, reduce the heat to medium-low and cook for 10 minutes.

Remove the lid and turn the heat up to high so the liquids can burn off. This step will help add a lovely colour to the chicken wings and will intensify the flavours of the finished dish.

In the meantime, pour the cup of water into the bowl in which you marinated the wings and loosen up any remaining bits. As the liquid in the pot burns off (you'll start seeing oil at the bottom of the pot), add the water. Quickly bring it to a boil then, with the lid on, reduce to a simmer.

Cook for 20 minutes and get ready to sample what I believe is the best way to enjoy chicken wings. Taste for salt and you can either leave gravy (great with rice, roti, Mac and Cheese or ground provisions) or burn off all the liquid for a more intense tasting dish.

You'll Need...

- Juice of 1 lime (to clean chicken)
- 3 lbs chicken wings
- 3/4 teaspoon salt
- 1 teaspoon ketchup
- 2 cloves garlic, crushed
- 1 teaspoon ginger, grated
- 1 each medium onion and tomato, chopped

- 1 tablespoon green seasoning
- 1/4 teaspoon black pepper
- 1/4 scotch bonnet pepper
- 1 scallion, chopped
- 2 sprigs thyme
- 2 tablespoons curry powder
- 2 tablespoons vegetable oil
- 1 tablespoon brown sugar
- 1 cup water

Scrumptious Island Stew Chicken with Chickpeas

This dish takes me back to when I first moved to Canada, and would hang out with my cousin and her husband at their house, working out and playing a bootleg copy of Tetris. My cousin usually had Stew Chicken with Chickpeas simmering on the stove. It was one of the few dishes that could instantly warm me during cold Canadian winters.

You'll Need...

- 4 lbs chicken, cut into serving size pieces
- Juice of 2 limes (to clean chicken)
- 1 teaspoon salt
- 1 teaspoon Worcestershire sauce
- 1 tablespoon ketchup
- 2 cloves garlic, crushed
- 1 teaspoon ginger, freshly grated
- 1 each medium onion and tomato, chopped
- Dash black pepper
- 1/4 scotch bonnet pepper
- 1 scallion, chopped
- 2 sprigs thyme
- 1/2 teaspoon green seasoning
- 2 tablespoons vegetable oil
- 1 heaping tablespoon brown sugar
- 1 oz (540 ml/194 fl) can chickpeas (channa)
- 1 cup water

Clean chicken according to the directions in the "Lime, Lemon or Vinegar!" section of the book. Place chicken pieces in large bowl and add all ingredients except oil, sugar, chickpeas and water. Marinate in the fridge for at least 2 hours.

Without discarding marinade bowl, stew according to steps 1-5 in the "Caramelized Chicken! Won't It Be Sweet?" section of the book. Bring to a boil then reduce heat to medium-low. Cover the pot and allow to cook for 15 minutes, stirring occasionally.

While this cooks, thoroughly rinse the canned chickpeas and empty into bowl with the leftover marinade. By this time, the chicken should have a rich brown colour.

Remove the lid, turn up heat to cook off the liquid that developed when the lid was on.

As soon as the liquid burns off, add the chickpeas with leftover marinade to the pot. Give it a good stir and add water. Bring this to a boil, cover the pot and reduce the heat to a simmer. Allow to cook for about 12 minutes. Stir and check to see if the gravy is runny or thick. If you find it too thin, turn up the heat and cook off some of the liquid.

Choose Your Cut: I use chicken legs since I love the flavour of dark meat.

Safety First: When adding the chicken to the pot, use a spoon with a long handle because the hot oil-sugar combo can cause some splattering.

Ultimate Trinbagonian Stew Chicken

When my daughters were much younger, my dad had a rhyme he would sing to them when they were sick. It went, "Chicken and rice makes everything nice." And, yes, grandma would be in the kitchen cooking Stew Chicken for them.

book. Season by adding everything except the oil, sugar and water. Mix and allow to marinate for a couple hours in the fridge.

Stew chicken according to steps 1-5 in the "Caramelized Chicken! Won't It Be Sweet?" section of the book but do not discard the marinade bowl yet. Turn the heat to medium-low, cover and allow to simmer for about 15 minutes. You'll notice that the chicken will spring some of its natural juices. Meanwhile, add the 1 1/2 cups of water to the bowl in which you marinated the chicken. Swish it around to pick up any marinade that may be stuck.

After about 15 minutes, remove the lid and turn up the heat to cook off all the liquid in the pot, which will give the chicken its final "brown" colour. This takes about 5 minutes and it's important to stir continuously so the chicken does not stick to the bottom of the pot. When all the liquid is gone, add the water you had sitting in the bowl. Stir and cook on medium heat for another 20-25 minutes. After 20 minutes, reduce the gravy to a thick consistency by turning up the heat and burning off excess liquid. Remember to check for salt before serving.

You'll Need...

- 4-5 lbs chicken
- Juice of 1 lime or lemon (to clean chicken)
- 1/2 tablespoon salt
- 1 teaspoon Worcestershire sauce
- 1 tablespoon ketchup
- 2 cloves garlic, thinly sliced
- 1 teaspoon ginger, grated
- 1 each medium onion and tomato, chopped

- 3 tablespoons shado beni, chopped
- 1/4 teaspoon black pepper
- 1/4 scotch bonnet pepper
- 1 scallion, chopped
- 2 sprigs thyme
- 1 small shallot
- 2 tablespoons vegetable oil
- 1 heaping tablespoon brown sugar
- 1 1/2 cups water

Clean chicken according to the directions in the "Lime, Lemon or Vinegar!" section of the

A Dash of Something Extra: If you can get Spanish thyme, add 1-2 finely chopped medium leaves to the chicken seasoning.

Choose Your Cut: I use a whole chicken that I divide into serving sized pieces. I like the mixture of dark and white meat. If using chicken breast, it's important that you allow the seasoned meat to marinate at least 3 hours to really infuse it and to help prevent it from drying out when cooked.

Caribbean-Inspired Chicken Lo Mein

The many cultures and people that make up the Caribbean melting pot heavily influence its cuisine. This Chicken Lo Mein is something I purchased after school from food trucks in San Fernando. Back then, the menu consisted of Fried Rice, Lo Mein or Chow Mein and Five-Spice Chicken. I'll never forget the unique Caribbean flavours added to these wonderful Chinese dishes.

You'll Need...

- 1 large onion
- 2 cloves garlic
- 1 tablespoon ginger, grated
- 1 carrot
- 1 1/2 cups different coloured bell peppers
- 2 chilli peppers
- 1 cup celery
- 1 cup broccoli
- Juice of 1/2 lime or lemon (to clean chicken)
- About 1 lb chicken breast
- 8 oz egg noodles
- 2 tablespoons vegetable oil
- 1/2 teaspoon salt
- 1 tablespoon oyster sauce
- 1 tablespoon soy sauce
- 2 tablespoons hoisin sauce
- 1-2 cups bok choy (pak choi)
- 2 scallions
- 2 cups bean sprouts (or cabbage)
- 1/2 teaspoon sesame oil

Wash and chop all vegetables. Thinly slice the chicken and clean according to the directions in the "Lime, Lemon or Vinegar!" section of the book. Also, cook your egg noodles according to package directions, drain and cool. This dish cooks very fast, so it's important to have everything prepped.

Heat your wok or large non-stick pan on medium-high and add the vegetable oil. Add sliced chicken and cook for about 4 minutes, stirring so it cooks evenly. Remove the pieces of chicken and set aside.

If your wok is dry, add a bit more oil. Still on medium-high heat, add the onion, garlic and grated ginger, and allow to cook for 1-2 minutes to release all their wonderful flavours. Add carrots, bell peppers, hot pepper, celery, broccoli and salt. Stir and cook for 2 minutes.

Meanwhile, in a small bowl, combine the oyster, soy and hoisin sauces. Add this mixture to the wok and stir then add the cooked chicken back to the wok. Stir in the bok choy and allow to cook for another minute before adding the cooked egg noodles. Give this a good stir to coat everything with the sauces.

Top with chopped scallions and bean sprouts, and cook for an additional minute, stirring continuously. Top with about 1/2 teaspoon of sesame oil for a bright finish and another layer of flavour. Check for salt and adjust accordingly.

Size Matters: Cut the vegetables the same size for uniform cooking.

Quantities: The recipe calls for 2 tablespoons of vegetable oil but after cooking the chicken, you may need to add an extra tablespoon. This depends on how seasoned your wok is or if you're using a non-stick pan.

Look For It: I use Guyanese-style Chow Mein egg noodles, which I find at the local West Indian store.

Simple Oven BBQ Chicken

This is not a dish you'd associate with the Caribbean, but it's my go-to when I feel like having juicy, seasoned chicken with a brilliant BBQ sauce glaze. This recipe is so simple that we're not even making the sauce. However, don't let its simplicity fool you into thinking it will lack flavour or originality. With cinnamon, allspice and fresh thyme, your kitchen will smell like heaven. I use Diana's Honey Garlic sauce (my Canadian friends will know it). With the addition of the honey and garlic flavours, this Simple Oven BBQ Chicken is unreal.

You'll Need...

- 1 (4-5 lb) chicken
- Juice of 1 lime or lemon (to clean chicken)
- 1 teaspoon salt
- 1 teaspoon black pepper
- 1/2 teaspoon cinnamon
- 1/2 teaspoon dry mustard
- 1/2 teaspoon allspice
- 4 sprigs thyme
- 1-2 cups your favourite BBQ sauce

Cut the chicken into four pieces or, if you are uncomfortable doing so, ask your butcher to do it for you. Alternatively, use already cut-up chicken parts. You'll be tempted to remove the chicken skin, but leave it on. The skin is a key factor to having tender and juicy chicken, so trim just the fat and excess skin. Clean chicken according to the directions in the "Lime, Lemon or Vinegar!" section of the book.

In a small bowl, mix the salt, black pepper, cinnamon, dry mustard, allspice and fresh thyme then coat all the pieces of chicken.

Place the seasoned chicken in a tin foil-lined baking dish on the middle rack of a 375 F-oven and cook for 40 minutes.

Tip the baking dish, and spoon out and discard any liquid and/or fat that may have accumulated. You need to get rid of all liquid so the BBQ sauce can really stick to the chicken for that gooey goodness. Using your favourite store-bought BBQ sauce, baste

the chicken pieces and place back in the oven for 10 minutes. Turn over the pieces of chicken and give the other side a nice coat of BBQ sauce. Put it back into the oven for another 10 minutes.

Flip over again and give the chicken a final generous coat of BBQ sauce, as you want the sauce to caramelize and form a sticky coating. Put the chicken back in the oven for a final 10 minutes. During the last 3 minutes, turn on the oven to broil to achieve the perfect colour.

Kick It Up: You can add some pepper sauce or freshly chopped scotch bonnet pepper to the marinating mix to give the chicken a wicked kick!

Moisture: If you're worried about the white meat going dry, rest assured that it won't. It will be the juiciest and most tender non-brined chicken breast that you'll ever have.

Island–Style Chicken Strips

Following the technique we'd use for making fried chicken when I was a kid (I still remember pounding the crackers in a tea towel to make the crumbs), these could easily be the best chicken strips you'll ever have. With a golden colour and specks of green herbs, they look stunning when they come out of the pan. You'll also be a superhero to your kids after you serve up a batch of these Island-Style Chicken Strips. But be warned, they won't want you to go back to the stuff you used to get them at fast food places.

You'll Need...

- 1 1/2 cup salted crackers crumbs
- 2 scallions
- 1 tablespoon thyme
- 1 tablespoon parsley
- About 1 lb chicken breast
- Juice of 1 lime (to clean chicken)
- 2 eggs
- 1/4 teaspoon sea salt
- 1/4 teaspoon black pepper
- 2-3 cups vegetable oil
- 3/4 cup all-purpose flour
- Sea salt (optional)

Place the crackers in a zip close plastic bag or in a tea towel and using a rolling pin, crush until you have the consistency of bread crumbs. I like texture, so I try to leave some of the crumbs a bit chunky. Set aside in a bowl.

Finely chop the scallions, thyme and parsley. Add the herbs to the bowl with the cracker crumbs and give it a good stir. I know this step is a bit strange to my Caribbean readers because rather than seasoning the chicken, as we traditionally would, we are seasoning the bread crumbs. But, stay with me.

Cut chicken into 1/4-inch strips and clean according to the directions in the "Lime, Lemon or Vinegar!" section of the book.

Crack both eggs into a bowl, toss in the black pepper and salt then give it a whisk.

Set up a batter and frying station. Arrange plates containing the flour, seasoned crumbs, chicken strips and egg wash. Also, ensure you have a paper towel-lined plate or a basket to drain the excess oil when the chicken strips are done. On medium-high, heat vegetable oil in a deep pan (I use a small wok so the oil doesn't splatter onto the stove while frying).

Take a piece of chicken, dust it in flour, dip into the eggs and drain off any excess, then roll in the seasoned bread crumbs. Repeat the process with three more chicken pieces before starting, so that you have a few to add to the hot oil at once. Don't overcrowd the pan or you risk your strips coming out soggy.

The oil should be hot by now, so gently place in each strip. Flip after a couple minutes and keep an eye on them. If you find the strips browning too fast, turn down your heat a bit. They take 5-7 minutes to fully cook and turn that lovely golden-brown colour. Drain on the paper towels and continue until all the chicken strips are cooked. While still hot, sprinkle with sea salt, if using.

Much like my Chicken Strips, after eating this Island-Style Fried Chicken you will never go back to fast food restaurants—not even during their 10-piece bucket sales. My grandmother handed down this recipe to me and over the years I've added personal touches to modify it to my daughters' tastes. These girls are picky eaters, so cooking for them can be challenging. I'm sure other parents can relate.

You'll Need...

- 5-6 lbs chicken pieces
- Juice of 2 limes or lemons (to clean chicken)
- 1 teaspoon pepper sauce
- 1/4 teaspoon black pepper
- 1/2 teaspoon ginger, freshly grated
- 1 teaspoon green seasoning
- 1 teaspoons salt
- About 2 1/2 cups vegetable oil
- 2 eggs

Dusting...
- 1-2 cups all-purpose flour
- 1 teaspoon paprika
- 1/4 teaspoon black pepper

Start by trying to pick chicken pieces that are all the same size, for even cooking time. Trim fat and excess skin, but do leave some on. I find the skin gives the meat a protective layer and prevents it from drying out while frying. You can remove it while you're eating. Clean chicken according to the directions in the "Lime, Lemon or Vinegar!" section of the book.

In a large bowl, season the chicken with the pepper sauce, black pepper, grated ginger, green seasoning and salt. Make sure to stir well then cover and allow to marinate in the fridge for about 2 hours.

In a heavy pan, heat the oil on medium-high. While the oil heats, you should do a couple of things. Crack the eggs into a small bowl and whisk, then add them to the bowl of seasoned chicken. Give it a good stir to get all the pieces of chicken coated in the eggs. Pour the flour onto a plate, add the paprika and black pepper, and mix well. Dust the pieces of chicken with the flour mixture.

Be sure to shake off any excess flour before placing pieces into the hot oil (and remember, it is hot oil that you're working with so be very careful). If your pan is not very large, fry 3 pieces at a time. Do not overcrowd the pan, as a reduction in oil temperature will lead to soggy chicken. Depending on the size of the chicken pieces and the cut (dark or white meat), cooking time will vary between 15-20 minutes. Since you're shallow frying, flip each piece every 4-5 minutes. If you find the outside turning brown fast, it likely means your oil is too hot. Adjust accordingly.

Have a wire tray or paper towel-lined basket ready to drain off any excess oil from the cooked pieces of chicken. Continue cooking in batches and remember to give the chicken a few minutes to cool before serving.

Crispy Chinese-Style Fried Chicken

I first tried this chicken at my Aunt Victoria's house in Trinidad. It was topped with a juice of lime pepper sauce, which had been marinating for a couple of months. The succulent pieces of chicken were just outstanding with the drops of spicy sauce, but the crispy skin stole the show. It's just one of those moments that will forever be engraved in my memory.

A Dash Of Something Extra: You can add 1/2 teaspoon of Chinese five-spice powder to the marinade for extra flavour and a little bit of finely chopped scotch bonnet pepper to add that "wickedness" to everything. You can also make a simple sauce by combining 1/4 cup hoisin sauce with 1 teaspoon good Caribbean pepper sauce.

Safety First: There is a simple way to figure out how much vegetable oil you'll need for frying so you won't have a dangerous mess of overflowing hot oil when you add the seasoned chicken to the pot. It will also help you determine how large of a pot you'll need. Before seasoning, place your chicken into the pot you plan on using to fry. Then, using a measuring cup, pour in water until the chicken is covered. Be sure to write down how many cups of water it took to completely cover the chicken. This is how much oil you will need. Once the chicken is covered, there should be three inches of space between the surface of the water and the rim of the pot.

Calling All Salt Lovers: Since you use soy sauce to marinate the chicken, you may find that it turns out a bit salty. That's why the recipe calls for light soy sauce. But, after marinating it overnight, you can certainly rinse the chicken with cool water. Keep in mind though that the sort of salty base is what's unique about this fried chicken.

You'll Need...

- 1 lime or lemon (to clean chicken)
- 1 (4-lb) chicken
- 1 1/2 cups light soy sauce
- 1 tablespoon fresh ginger
- Vegetable oil (see Keep It Safe note)

Clean chicken according to the directions in the "Lime, Lemon or Vinegar!" section of the book. Place in a large, zip close, plastic bag. Put the bagged chicken in a bowl that can fit in your fridge so if the bag leaks, you won't have a mess in your fridge. Pour in the soy sauce and grate the ginger directly into the bag. When you seal the bag, squeeze out as much air as possible. Then, massage the chicken so the marinade gets up close and personal with the entire bird.

Allow the seasoned chicken to marinate in the fridge overnight. When ready to cook, remove from the fridge and allow to come back to room temperature as you heat the oil for frying (get it to about 325 F).

Using paper towels, dry off the chicken and gently add it to the hot oil. Depending on the size of your chicken, it can take 20-30 minutes to cook all the way through and produce that lovely, crispy skin. If you're using chicken pieces, they should be fully cooked in about 20 minutes. Place the fried chicken on a cooling rack in a baking tray so the excess oil can drain off.

Geera Chicken

Since the meat traditionally used in this dish is pork (see recipe on page 56), this one is for all the pork haters. Geera (cumin) creates a strong spice base for this "bar food", which is similar to Spanish tapas. The garlic, herbs and hot peppers give it that unique Caribbean kick.

and release its full bouquet.

Add the seasoned chicken to the pot and stir. The idea is to coat all the pieces with some of that lovely paste you created and to pick up all the bits from the bottom of the pan (similar to deglazing).

Turn the heat to medium-high and cover the pot with a lid. The chicken will come to a boil and start releasing some natural juices. When it does, turn the heat back down and allow to cook for about 10 minutes. Check occasionally and stir. If for some reason there's no liquid, add a bit of water to allow the chicken to fully cook. Since you're using chicken breast, you don't want to overcook and risk it going dry.

There should still be some liquid in the pot after 10 minutes, so remove the lid and turn up the heat a bit. The idea is to burn off all that liquid and, in doing so, give the pieces of chicken a lovely coating of all the spices and seasoning you used. It should take about 3-4 minutes to completely burn off

You'll Need...

- 2 lbs boneless, skinless chicken breast
- 1/2 lime or lemon (to clean chicken)
- 1 teaspoon salt
- 1/4 teaspoon black pepper
- 2 scallions, chopped
- 2 heaping tablespoons cilantro with stems, chopped
- 1 scotch bonnet pepper, diced
- 4 sprigs thyme
- 2 tablespoons vegetable oil
- 1/2 large onion, sliced
- 4 cloves garlic, sliced
- 1 tablespoon ground roasted cumin

Cut the chicken into 1-inch cubes and

clean according to the directions in the "Lime, Lemon or Vinegar!" section of the book. In a bowl, season with salt, black pepper, diced scallions, chopped cilantro, chopped scotch bonnet pepper and thyme. Give it a good stir and leave it to marinate for about 30 minutes.

In a fairly deep saucepan, heat the vegetable oil on medium-high then add the sliced onion and garlic. Turn down the heat and cook for about 4 minutes, stirring often, until the onion is soft. Add the ground roasted cumin to the pot and stir. It will go grainy and darker. That is normal. Make sure the heat is on low and cook for 3-4 minutes. What you're doing is allowing the roasted cumin to toast

Authenticity: Traditionally, shado beni is used instead of cilantro. But as I've mentioned, cilantro is a good substitute when you can't source shado beni.

A Dash of Something Extra: If you want to use the whole cumin seed—roasting it in a dry pan on high heat then grinding—you'll heighten the overall flavour of this dish. But be prepared for your entire house to be encased in that strong cumin smell.

Grilled Five-Spice Chicken

This Grilled Five-Spice Chicken is inspired by the huge Chinese influence—especially on our everyday cuisine—in the Caribbean.

You'll Need...

- 4 lbs chicken thighs
- Juice of 1 lime (to clean chicken)
- 1/2 scotch bonnet pepper, de-seeded
- 2 scallions
- 3 cloves garlic
- 2 teaspoons ginger, freshly grated
- 1 tablespoon vinegar
- 1 tablespoon soy sauce
- 1 tablespoon five-spice powder

Keeping some of the skin on the chicken to help it stay moist as it grills, clean chicken according to the directions in the "Lime, Lemon or Vinegar!" section of the book. I use chicken thighs, as I love this piece of dark meat because it absorbs marinades well.

Chop the scotch bonnet pepper and scallion very finely and crush the garlic as smoothly as you can. For the garlic, I use my mortar and pestle, and employ a pinch of salt to help create a paste.

Add everything, including the chicken pieces, into a strong zip close, plastic, freezer bag that won't leak or break. Try to get as much air as possible out of the bag and quickly seal it. Once it's sealed, massage the chicken and marinade by moving it around with your hands. Place the bag in the fridge for at least 3 hours.

15 minutes before you fire up the grill, take the bag with the marinating chicken out of the fridge so it comes back to room temperature.

Your grill should be between 375 and 400 F. Place the chicken on the grill, skin side up to start. Flip every 4-5 minutes, making sure to look for flare-ups when it's skin side down, and cook for about 25-30 minutes. Alternatively, you can make this dish in the oven. To do so, preheat the oven to 375 F, place the chicken on a wire rack in a baking tray (so it's not sitting in its own fat) and cook for about 40-45 minutes. You may need to turn on your broiler for the last 5 minutes to get that lovely golden colour.

Allow the chicken pieces to rest for five minutes before serving so the meat relaxes and you get that true juiciness from the five-spice marinade.

History Lesson: Between 1853 and 1879, 14,000 Chinese labourers, bound for the sugar plantations, were brought to the British Caribbean as part of a larger system of contract labour. These Chinese labourers settled in three main locations: Jamaica, Trinidad and British Guiana (now Guyana).

Kick It Up: Because I love the vibe, I use fresh scotch bonnet pepper. But you can certainly use one teaspoon of hot sauce.

Imagine unveiling this chicken as friends arrive at your backyard get-together. They'll be blown away. Also, be prepared for your neighbours to first peek over the fence to investigate the amazing aroma and then invite themselves over to try your creation!

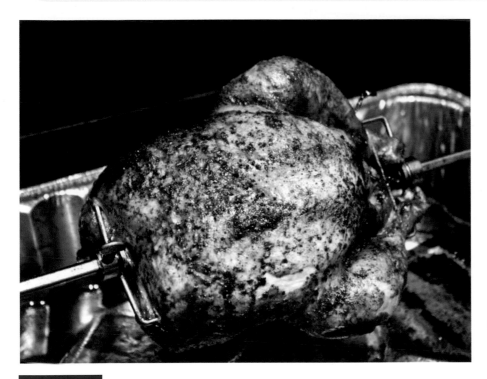

You'll Need...

- **Zest 1 lime**
- **1/4 teaspoon cinnamon**
- **1/4 teaspoon allspice**
- **1/2 teaspoon salt**
- **1/4 teaspoon black pepper**
- **1/4 teaspoon onion powder**
- **1 teaspoon brown sugar**
- **1 whole (4-lb) chicken**
- **4 sprigs thyme**
- **1 scallion**
- **Juice 1 lemon**
  (to clean chicken)

Rub: Grate lime zest into a bowl then add all the other dry ingredients (except the thyme, scallion and lemon) and give it a good stir.

Clean chicken according to the directions in the "Lime, Lemon or Vinegar!" section of the book. Before using the dry rub, open up the cavity of the bird, and add the thyme, scallion and lemon halves. Then, evenly coat the chicken in the dry rub.

After doing so, it's important that you truss the chicken (tie with string) so it's compact and will not toss around as it does its thing on the rotisserie. Cover with plastic wrap, place in the fridge and allow to marinate for about 30 minutes or so.

Preheat your grill at 300 F. Put chicken on rotisserie, cover the lid and let it cook for 2 hours. After the first hour, the chicken will start to develop colour and the scent will start to really make its presence known. Do remember to keep the heat constant and keep filling the drip pan with water (see Flare-Up note). After an hour and a half turn the heat to 400 F to ensure the chicken is fully cooked inside and to give it that appealing colour rotisserie chicken should have.

After 2 hours, your rotisserie chicken should be ready to join the party. Remove from the heat and allow to rest, covered with tin foil, for about 15 minutes before cutting.

Kick It Up: If you want to kick this up a bit, you can finely dice a scotch bonnet pepper and add it to the rub.

Prevent Flare-Ups: Place a disposable pan with about half an inch of water directly below where the chicken will be on the grill. As the rotisserie chicken cooks, it will drop fat and this pan with water will prevent flare-ups.

Alternative Cooking Method: You can make this chicken in a roasting pan in the oven. Place the chicken on a wire rack in the pan, so it's not sitting in the fat and oil that will be released. Roast at 375 F for 2 hours. However, cooking it on the grill with the rotisserie is ideal, as the fat will self-baste the chicken before falling into the pan below it.

If you're not familiar with Chicken Lollipops, they're the drumettes of the wing that have been shaped to look like the favourite childhood treat. I decided to make a rub to marinate Chicken Lollipops using ingredients that islanders employ on a daily basis.

according to the directions in the "Lime, Lemon or Vinegar!" section of the book.

In a small bowl, combine all remaining ingredients and give the mixture a good whisk. Pour the marinade over the trimmed and shaped chicken pieces and combine well—get your hands in there. Cover with plastic wrap and place in the fridge to marinate for 1-3 hours then bring back to room temperature while your grill heats up. Do not discard the marinade bowl yet.

Grill as you normally do chicken—at 375 F for about 30 minutes. Rotate lollipops every 4-5 minutes and baste with the leftover marinade from the bowl in which they marinated. As they cook and the heat of the grill intensifies, you'll start getting that lovely aroma of the marinade—especially the curry powder! Keep an eye on the lollipops so they don't overcook and dry out, but be sure to get some grill marks on them to really deepen the rich flavours with which you infused them.

You'll Need...

- Juice of 1 lime or lemon
  (to clean chicken)
- 5 lbs chicken drumsticks
- 1 tablespoon curry powder
- 1 teaspoon salt
- 1/4 teaspoon black pepper
- 1 teaspoon brown sugar
- 1/2 teaspoon mustard powder
- 1 tablespoon parsley, chopped
- 1 teaspoon thyme
- 1 tablespoon soy sauce
- 2 tablespoons rum
- 2 crushed cloves garlic
- 1 teaspoon paprika and onion powder

To shape the lollipops: After removing the skin, firmly grab the thin end of the drumstick then carefully cut through the meat surrounding the bone. Use a sawing motion and turn the drumstick all the way around as you cut. Try not to force it, letting the knife do the work instead. Be sure to look out for the tiny long bone that will be close to the drumstick's main bone. Once the meat is cut, use your knife to scrape the meat from the bone, pushing it down to the other end. You may need to cut through a couple of sinews. You should have what looks like a handle with a ball of chicken meat at one end.

With drumsticks shaped into lollipops, clean

Be Thrifty: Traditionally, the drummette part of chicken wings is used to make the lollipop shape, but I use chicken drumsticks. There's more meat and it's much cheaper than purchasing chicken wings.

Keep It Simple: There's no need for any barbecue sauce on these or you'll destroy all the work you did to create that lovely exotic flavour from the curry powder, spices and herbs. However, the Tamarind BBQ Sauce on page 127 would make an excellent dipping sauce.

Apple-Mango Chicken Salad

I'll be the first to admit that I'm no fan of chicken breast or "chicken chess", as we sometimes say in the Caribbean. So, this recipe came about out of the necessity to use the breast after having roasted chicken for dinner. Now we purposely buy chicken breast because this Apple-Mango Chicken Salad is so outstanding that it's one of the few dishes everyone in my household can agree on! Cooking for teenagers can be a bit tricky at times.

With most things I prepare, I like to incorporate a bit of the islands. So, the addition of the ripe mango and a pinch of curry powder was only natural.

Wash, peel and dice the mango then wash and dice the apple. There's no need to peel the apple, as the skin gives it some extra texture. Pour the lemon juice over the diced apple to prevent it from discolouring. Dice the celery and onion a bit smaller than the apple and mango.

Place the shredded chicken in a deep bowl, add all the other ingredients and give it a good mix. Chill in the fridge for about 30 minutes before serving in a sandwich.

Kick It Up: Try to get a mango that's about 90 per cent ripe, so it's firm. This will make it easy to dice and handle in general. If you don't have red onion, any sweet or mild onion will work. The idea is to not have karate breath after eating this. If you're daring, be sure to add some pepper sauce or some finely chopped scotch bonnet pepper for that extra kick!

Serve and Store: This recipe makes enough Apple-Mango Chicken Salad for about five to eight sandwiches, depending on how generous you are. It can keep in the fridge for about two days. If you store it, you may notice some liquid develops in the container. Just give it a stir and you're good to go.

You'll Need...

- 1/2 cup mango
- 1/2 cup apple
- 1 teaspoon lemon juice
- 1/2 cup celery
- 1/4 cup red onion
- 3 cups oven-roasted chicken, shredded
- 3/4 cup mayo
- 3/4 teaspoon prepared mustard
- Pinch each salt, black pepper, curry powder

Jerk Chicken Wraps

These Jerk Chicken Wraps are excellent as everyday sandwiches for your family or for guests, who will make a dash for the platter when you present them at your next gathering. You'll be astonished at how juicy the jerk chicken is. And with the fresh tropical fruit flavours, your taste buds will go into overdrive. You can make these ahead of time, cover with plastic wrap and store in the fridge.

You'll Need...

- 3 lbs boneless chicken breast
- Juice of 1 lemon (to clean chicken)
- 1 1/2 cups jerk marinade
- 1 tablespoon vegetable oil
- 1 1/2 cups carrots, julienned
- 1 1/2 cups lettuce
- 1 1/2 cup firm mango, julienned
- 1 1/2 cups pineapple chunks
- 1 1/2 cups cucumber ribbons
  (use a potato peeler)
- About 8-10 (10-inch) flour tortillas

Garlicky Spread...
- 2 (8-oz) containers plain Greek yogurt
- 1 cucumber; peeled, seeded and diced
- 1 tablespoon olive oil
- Juice of 1/2 lemon
- Salt and pepper, to taste
- 1 tablespoon dill, chopped
- 3 cloves garlic
- Few drops honey (optional)

Garlicky Spread: In a food processor or blender, combine yogurt, cucumber, olive oil, lemon juice, salt, pepper, dill, garlic and honey (if using). Process until well combined then transfer to a separate dish, cover and refrigerate for at least one hour for best flavour.

Clean chicken according to the directions in the "Lime, Lemon or Vinegar!" section of the book. Place in a bowl, cover in jerk marinade and allow it to marinate for at least 1 hour.

In the meantime, move your oven rack so it's about 6-8 inches away from the main heat source and set oven to the broil setting. Line a baking pan with tin foil and brush it with oil or use cooking spray. Place the chicken on the pan, cover in remaining marinade and broil for 10 minutes. Remove from the oven, flip over and broil for another 8 minutes. If you're using thick chicken breast, broil an additional 4 minutes. Set aside to cool.

Blanch the carrots by bringing to a boil about 3 cups of water and tossing them in for 25 seconds. Immediately, transfer to a bowl with ice water to stop cooking process. Drain and pat dry with paper towels. Shred the lettuce.

When the chicken is cool, slice into 1/4-inch strips and if you have any drippings in the baking pan, pour over the sliced chicken and give it a good mix.

Take a flour tortilla and spread about a teaspoon of the Garlicky Spread across a 1-inch strip the length of the tortilla. Across one end, place a bit of the chicken, mango, pineapple, lettuce and cucumber ribbons, and roll tightly, tucking everything in as you do so. Slice in the middle so you have two pieces of Jerk Chicken Wrap. You'll need toothpicks to hold these together.

Time-Saver: I use my favourite packaged jerk marinade and suggest you do the same to save time.

Traditionalists feel jerked meat must be done over pimento wood. Though I agree that there is a unique taste from the smoke of pimento wood, when you can't source it you must rely on a bold jerk marinade to compensate and help maximize flavour.

These Jerk Pork Sliders are guaranteed to excite your taste buds with the brightness of the scotch bonnet pepper and the earthy goodness of the allspice, cinnamon and nutmeg. With the unique punch of the jerk marinade infusion, you will have friends and family begging you for the recipe.

then, on the wrap, make a log with the now-seasoned meat. Try to shape it about 1/4-inch bigger in circumference than the size of your buns because it will shrink as it grills. Roll and shape as you wrap in cling wrap until you have a thick, sausage-like roll. Seal the ends and place in the freezer to set. It may take a couple of hours.

Wet a sharp knife for easier slicing. Slice meat, now in log form, to the thickness you want.

Grill as you would normally grill burgers—covered, over medium heat for 4-5 minutes on each side or until a meat thermometer reads 160 F.

You'll Need...

- 1/2 scotch bonnet pepper (or any hot pepper you like)
- 1 scallion
- 2 sprigs thyme
- 1 clove garlic
- 1 teaspoon allspice
- 1/4 teaspoon cinnamon
- 1/4 teaspoon nutmeg
- 1/4 teaspoon black pepper
- 1/4 teaspoon sea salt
- 1 teaspoon brown sugar
- 1 tablespoon white vinegar
- 1 tablespoon lime juice
- 1 teaspoon soy sauce
- 1 tablespoon orange juice
- 1/4 teaspoon grated ginger
- 1 lb ground pork

Give the scallion, scotch bonnet pepper and thyme a rough chop. If the stem of the thyme is not tender, remove the little leaves and discard stem. Add all your ingredients, except the ground pork, into a blender and work until you have a smooth consistency.

Place the ground pork in a deep bowl and cover with marinade. Work until everything's well incorporated. Place a sheet of cling wrap on a flat surface

Substitute: You can use ground chicken, beef or turkey if you don't dine with the swine.

The Only One: After you place each patty on a toasted bun, top it with a Caribbean salsa. This can be made by combining equal parts avocado, tomato and mango with diced red onion, 1 tablespoon cilantro, sea salt and black pepper to taste. Drizzle the salsa with extra virgin olive oil and some organic honey. There's no need for other condiments, as the salsa will have a rich creaminess from the ripe avocado and the pieces of ripe mango will explode in your mouth with every bite.

Tantalizing Trini
Geera Pork

Prior to making this recipe, I only ate Geera Pork once—out of respect for an island host who served it. That's because I wasn't really a fan of geera (cumin). But I love the way my recipe turned out and it actually made me change my mind about cumin. It seems yuh boy have sweet hand after all...

You'll Need...

- 3 lbs pork
- 2 tablespoons lime or lemon juice (to clean meat)
- 1 medium tomato, diced
- 1 teaspoon salt
- 1/8 teaspoon black pepper
- 1/4 teaspoon curry powder
- 2 small onions, sliced and divided
- 1 tablespoon green seasoning
- 4 leaves shado beni, chopped
- 1 scotch bonnet pepper
- 2 tablespoons vegetable oil
- 4 garlic cloves, crushed
- 1 heaping tablespoon roasted cumin powder
- 2 cups water

Cut pork into small pieces, about 3/4-inch thick, and place in a bowl. Clean pork according to the directions in the "Lime, Lemon or Vinegar!" section of the book. Add the tomato, salt, black pepper, curry powder, 1 sliced onion, green seasoning, shado beni and scotch bonnet pepper. Yes, you're using a whole pepper for this one because this dish is known for being extra hot. You can adjust to your own tolerance. Give this a stir and let it marinate in the fridge for a couple of hours.

Heat the oil on medium-high, add the remaining sliced onion and garlic then turn heat to low and allow that to cook for 4-5 minutes or until the edges start to go brown. Add the roasted cumin powder and cook for a few more minutes. The mixture should begin to thicken and

start sticking to the bottom of the pot—that's normal. The aroma will be intense, but wonderful!

To the pot, add a few pieces of seasoned pork at a time and stir as you go. You want to coat the meat with the cumin paste. After adding all the pork, bring it up to a boil then lower the heat and, with the lid on, allow to cook for about 20 minutes. The pork will spring its own natural juices.

After 20 minutes, turn the heat to high and cook off all the liquid. It will take about 5 minutes. Try to make sure the bottom of the pot is completely dry then add 2 cups of water and bring to a boil. Cover the pot, lower to a gentle simmer and allow to cook for another 45 minutes. If you find that the pork is tender enough after this time, turn up the heat and allow the remaining liquid to burn off. This dish is usually served without any gravy, but I love me some gravy so I don't cook off all the liquid.

BBQ Pigtails is one of the less glamorous dishes to come out of the Caribbean. To be honest, the first time I saw it being grilled in Barbados a few years back, I was a bit apprehensive. Don't get me wrong, I love salted pigtails stewed or in soups, but I found the whole grilling idea a bit weird. Luckily, I don't discriminate when it comes to food, so it was only a matter of time before this piggy dish made its way onto my grill.

You'll Need...

- Juice of 1 lime or lemon (to clean meat)
- 2 lbs salted pigtails
- 1 tablespoon green seasoning
- 1/2 cup your favourite BBQ sauce

Scrape pigtails with a knife and keep an eye out for any hairs, which you'll remove. Clean pork according to the directions in the "Lime, Lemon or Vinegar!" section of the book. Place in a deep pot, cover with water and bring to a boil. Allow this to cook on a rolling boil for 45 minutes.

Drain and rinse with clean water. Place the pigtails back in the pot, top with water and bring to a boil again. As the water starts to boil, add the green seasoning (or any seasoning and herbs you like). By doing so, you're infusing the pigtails with additional flavours. Boil for 50 minutes. This will remove the salt in which the pigtails were cured and help to tenderize the meat. Discard the water but don't rinse the meat, as you want the green seasoning to remain on the pigtails.

Place on a 375-400 F grill. Keep an eye on the pigtails, as it's easy for them to

char with all the skin and fat. After a couple of minutes, you can start liberally brushing on your favourite BBQ sauce. Turn the heat down a bit, as you really want to develop some caramelized flavours. During the cooking process, which should take about 15 minutes, keep flipping and brushing with BBQ sauce. With all the pre-boiling, the meat will be falling off the bone. The sweetness from the caramelized BBQ sauce and the open flame of the grill will infuse a wonderful flavour to the salty undertones of the brine in which these pigtails were originally cured.

A good friend from Grenada passed this recipe onto me about 20 years ago. One plate and you'll know why Grenadians are so passionate about their Oil Down and why they refer to it as their national dish. You will notice that there are some minor differences between the traditional way it is cooked and the way I make it. But as with everything, I've added my own personal touches.

If you're wondering, the name Oil Down comes from the fact that the oil from the coconut milk coats and flavours this dish like no other.

You'll Need...

- 2 lbs salted pigtails
- Juice of 1 lemon (to clean chicken)
- 3 lbs chicken breast
- 1 teaspoon green seasoning
- 1/4 teaspoon black pepper
- 2 tablespoons olive oil
- 1 large breadfruit
- 1 large carrot
- 2 cups pumpkin
- 4 green cooking bananas
- 6 eddoes
- 2 cups dasheen leaves
- 1 onion, chopped
- 3 cloves garlic, crushed
- 2 scallions
- 3 pimento peppers
- 2 tablespoons parsley, chopped
- 2 tablespoons shado beni, chopped
- 4 sprigs thyme
- 1 scotch bonnet pepper
- 1/2 teaspoon curry powder
- 3/4 teaspoon turmeric (sorfran)
- 3 cups coconut milk

Cut the salted pigtails into 1 1/2-inch pieces, place in a deep pot, cover with water and bring to a boil. Reduce to a rolling boil for about 40 minutes. This will not only help tenderize the salted pigtails, but also remove most of that harsh salt in which they were cured. Drain, rinse and set aside.

Clean chicken according to the directions in the "Lime, Lemon or Vinegar!" section of the book". Season with the green seasoning and black pepper, and allow to marinate while the pigtails pre-cook. You can also peel, wash and cube into large pieces the breadfruit, carrot, pumpkin, cooking bananas, eddoes and dasheen leaves. So they don't discolour, make sure to keep the vegetables and provisions in a bowl covered with water.

In a deep pot, heat the vegetable oil on medium. Add the onion, garlic, scallions and pimento peppers and cook about 2 minutes.

Turn the heat down to low and begin to stack everything in the pot. Layer in the now pre-cooked salted pigtails, seasoned chicken and everything else, except curry powder, turmeric and coconut milk.

Mix the curry powder and turmeric with the coconut milk and pour into the pot. With the lid on, turn the heat up to bring the contents of the pot to a boil. Then, reduce to a simmer, leave the lid slightly ajar and cook for about 35-40 minutes. Try not to stir, as you really don't want things to fall apart and become mush.

Hold The Salt: You'll notice that I didn't add any salt, so you'll have to adjust accordingly. The remaining salt in the pigtails should be enough to properly season the dish, but everyone's tolerance is different.

Personalize: You can personalize Oil Down by adding your favourite ground provision like yams, dasheen and cassava. You can also add smoked herring and saltfish. Flour dumplings are also included for that unique Grenadian way.

Substitute: If you can't get dasheen leaves, you can use Jamaican callaloo or regular spinach.

Braised-in-Guinness Oxtail

This is absolutely one of the best oxtail recipes I've created. Though the oxtail-Guinness combination is not something that comes to mind when you think about Caribbean cuisine, I assure you this will be a hit.

You'll Need...

- 3 lbs oxtail, cut and trimmed of excess fat
- Juice of 1 lemon (to clean meat)
- 2 tablespoons vegetable oil
- 1 large onion
- 1 1/2 cups celery, diced
- 1/2 teaspoon black pepper
- 1/2 teaspoon oregano
- 4 sprigs thyme
- 1 can (156 ml) tomato paste
- 2 large carrots, cut into chunks
- 2 bay leaves
- 1 teaspoon salt
- 2 cans Guinness
- 1 scotch bonnet pepper (optional)
- 1 cup water

Clean meat according to the directions in the "Lime, Lemon or Vinegar!" section of the book. Heat the oil in a deep, heavy pan on medium-high and brown the oxtail pieces. Try not to crowd the pan or the meat will release moisture and boil instead of brown. Remember to keep turning the pieces of oxtail. After browning, which should take 10-15 minutes, remove the oxtail pieces and set aside.

Turn the heat to very low, and add the onion, celery, black pepper, oregano and thyme (leave on the stem, as you can remove it later). Allow this to cook for about 3-5 minutes. Add the tomato paste and give it a good stir. You're trying to release the natural sugars in the tomato paste and create a rich base. You'll notice that the mixture will go darker and there will be a lovely scent in your kitchen. Cook, stirring continuously, for about 2-3 minutes.

Return oxtail to the pot, then add carrots, bay leaves and salt. Give that a stir, turn the heat to high and add the 2 cans of Guinness. Stir well and, with the lid on the pot, bring to a boil. Once boiling, turn the heat to low and cook for about 20 minutes. If using, add the whole scotch bonnet pepper to the pot.

Add the water, bring back up to a boil then reduce to low again. Allow to cook for about 3 hours or until the meat starts falling off the bone. While cooking, stir every 15 minutes and if you notice you're running low on liquid, add a bit more water. After 3 hours, take out the sprigs of thyme and the hot pepper. With the pot uncovered, turn up the heat to thicken the rich gravy.

Heat Control: Hot pepper is optional, but I love the additional flavour. Remember to keep it whole, as you're using it for flavour, not heat. If you do want the excitement of heat, burst it open near the end of cooking.

The Beer In Here: I use Guinness Draught but I know we get the extra stout version in the Caribbean, which is a bit stronger. Rest assured that the alcohol will burn off.

A Dash Of Something Extra: If you want a bit more Caribbean influence, add a few pimento berries to the pot and 1/2 teaspoon of green seasoning.

The Ultimate Curry Goat

I was never a fan of curry goat. I'm sure I can count on my fingers the number of times I've had it. But after perfecting this recipe, I must confess that I've outdone myself and have developed a new appreciation for this dish. For the great cook that my mom is—and I guess I can add my sisters and aunts to the list—I think I've trumped them all. Just don't tell them I said that because it will lead to... problems.

You'll Need...

- 2 lbs goat, cut into 1-inch pieces
- Juice of 1 lemon (to clean meat)
- 3/4 teaspoon salt
- Dash black pepper
- 3 sprigs thyme
- 1 tomato, sliced
- 2 scallions
- 1/2 teaspoon curry powder
- 1/4 teaspoon cumin
- 1/4 teaspoon amchar masala (optional)
- 1 leaf Spanish thyme, crushed (optional)
- 4 leaves shado beni, chopped
- 1/2 teaspoon ketchup
- 3 tablespoons vegetable oil
- 1 medium onion, sliced
- 3 cloves garlic, crushed
- 1/2 scotch bonnet pepper
- 1 1/2 tablespoons curry powder
- 3 1/4 cups water

Clean the goat according to the directions in the "Lime, Lemon or Vinegar!" section of the book. Season with all ingredients except the oil, onion, garlic, hot pepper, 1 1/2 tablespoons of curry powder and water. Mix well, cover and put in the fridge to marinate for at least 2 hours.

In a heavy pot, heat the oil on medium-high then add the onion and garlic, and allow to cook for a few minutes (until onion is soft and garlic releases its flavours). Add the hot pepper and curry powder to the onion and garlic. Give this a minute or two, until it starts to stick or go really thick. Add 1/4 cup of water and allow to cook on medium heat for about 5 minutes, stirring continuously.

As the water dries off, you'll notice the curry will take on a sort of grainy texture and the oil at the bottom of the pot will start to become visible again. This is a good sign. Turn up the heat and start adding to the pot a few seasoned goat pieces at a time, stirring between each batch. This will ensure each piece is coated with the curry base. After you've added all the meat, cover the pot and bring to a boil then lower the heat and allow to cook, on a gentle simmer, for 25 minutes.

Remove the lid and turn the heat up to burn off all the liquid. Add the remaining 3 cups of water and bring that to a boil. Once it's boiling, cover the pot with the lid, turn down the heat to low and simmer, stirring every 15 minutes

or so. You're basically braising the meat so it's nice and tender with a rich, thick gravy. This can take up to 1 1/2–2 hours, depending on how tender you like your meat. Once you're happy with its texture, reduce the gravy to a thickness you like. Usually the gravy will be perfect, but if you find that it's a bit runny, raise the heat and burn off some liquid.

Time-Saver: After you add the three cups of water, feel free to use a pressure cooker to drastically cut back the cooking time. I've also seen my aunt do this step in the oven. She puts the Curry Goat in a baking dish, covers with tin foil, and sets the oven at about 375 F.

Lamb Chops Braised In Coconut-Curry Sauce

Lamb wasn't a very popular choice when I was a young fella. Quite honestly, my mom never made it. Back then, goat was the champ when it came to a good curry. Also, in those days, lamb was not as readily available on the islands as it is today. So, it's only now that curry lamb is gaining popularity throughout the Caribbean.

The tender pieces of lamb, cooked in a coconut-curry sauce are outstanding as a partner for roti, ground provisions, rice, dumplings or even something as simple as a side salad.

You'll Need...

- 5 lamb chops (about 3 lbs)
- Juice of 1 lemon (to clean meat)
- 2 tablespoons vegetable oil
- 1 shallot (or onion), finely chopped
- 3 cloves garlic, crushed
- 1 teaspoon ginger
- 1 1/2 tablespoons curry powder
- 1 tablespoon shado beni, chopped
- 1/4 scotch bonnet pepper, de-seeded and finely chopped
- 2 scallions, chopped
- 1 tablespoon fresh thyme
- 1/4 teaspoon black pepper
- 1/2 teaspoon salt
- 1 1/2 cups coconut milk
- 1 cup water
- 2 tablespoons chopped flat leaf parsley
- 8 grape tomatoes

Clean lamb according to the directions in the "Lime, Lemon or Vinegar!" section of the book and pat dry. On medium, heat the oil in a deep and heavy saucepan. Add the chops and sear for a few minutes, turning so they brown on each side. Remove and set aside.

Turn heat to low and add 1 more tablespoon of oil, if necessary. Toss in the diced shallot (or onion), crushed garlic and grate the ginger directly into the pot. Let that cook on low for about 3 minutes, stirring so you create a wonderful flavour base. Add the curry powder and cook for a couple minutes, stir well. It will go grainy and darker as it cooks.

Add the chops, and any liquid that may have accumulated on the plate on which you had them, back to the saucepan. Move chops around to pick up some of that curry base.

Toss in the chopped shado beni, scotch bonnet pepper, scallions, thyme and black pepper. Give it a good stir then add the salt, coconut milk and water. Turn the heat up and bring to a boil then reduce the heat to very low so you have a gentle simmer. Cover the pot with its lid and, stirring every 10 minutes, let that cook for about 1 1/2 hours or until the

lamb is tender and falling off the bone.

You may need to personalize this dish. I like my gravy thick, so I turn up the heat to burn off most excess liquid. When the gravy is as thick as you want, toss in the chopped parsley and the grape tomatoes. Turn off heat and cover the pot for 3 minutes. Check the dish to ensure it has enough salt for your liking.

Substitute: If you don't have grape tomatoes, chop up a medium tomato.

Cowheel Soup

Ladies and gents, I must confess that I'm not a fan of Cowheel (cow foot or bull foot) Soup. So, were it up to me, this recipe would not be here because I don't normally cook it. However, my mom asked, in her Trinbagonian accent, "Son, yuh eh doing ah Cowheel Soup?" According to her, it's one of the best soups we have in the Caribbean and should be included in any book documenting our cuisine.

You'll Need...

- 1 tablespoon vegetable oil
- 1 large onion, diced
- 2 cloves garlic, crushed
- 4 pimento peppers (optional)
- 4 sprigs thyme
- 1/2 teaspoon black pepper
- 2 lbs cowheel
- 1 cup yellow split peas
- 1 teaspoon salt
- 2 carrots, cut into big pieces
- 12-16 cups water
- 1 scotch bonnet pepper
- 8-10 okra
- 3 potatoes, cut in quarters
- 2 scallions, chopped
- 1 cup pumpkin, diced

Dumplings...
- 1 cup all-purpose flour
- Pinch salt
- Water

On medium, heat the vegetable oil in a deep pot. Add the diced onion, garlic, pimento peppers, thyme and black pepper, and cook for 3-5 minutes. Add the cowheel and stir well. Add the yellow split peas, salt and carrots, stir and cover with water. Raise the heat to high and bring to a boil then reduce to a simmer.

Cook for about 2 hours. As the soup simmers, drop in the whole scotch bonnet pepper. Also, if you notice foam gather at the top of the pot, skim and discard.

After 2 hours, the peas should be tender enough to start thickening the soup. The pieces of cowheel will also be tender, so add the okra, potatoes, chopped scallions and pumpkin. Allow to simmer for 30 minutes.

Meanwhile, in a small bowl prepare the dumplings by combining the flour, pinch of salt and enough water to form a soft but firm-to-the-touch dough. Cover with plastic wrap and let rest for 15 minutes.

During the last 10 minutes of cooking, pinch off small pieces of dough and roll between your hands to form small cigars. Add to the pot and let cook for the final 10 minutes.

During the last 4 minutes of cooking, taste for salt and adjust accordingly. Once soup cooks, fish out sprigs of thyme and scotch bonnet pepper. If you're like me and like kick though, burst the scotch bonnet pepper in the pot and enjoy the explosive flavour.

At The Butcher's: Make sure your butcher cleans and cuts the cowheel into small pieces.

Size Matters: You will definitely need a large pot because Caribbean soup always turns out to be a huge feast. There will be enough here for at least 8 people as a main dish.

When you grow up on the islands, at one point or another, you've had canned corned beef. And, no, it's not the sliced stuff you get on rye bread at North American delis. We've reinvented the use of canned corned beef with the many ways we've perfected preparing it in its simple glory.

It had been a couple decades since I last had Corned Beef with Cabbage and I almost forgot its preparation method. I was visiting my parents when they mentioned that they had this dish for dinner a few nights earlier and a rush of memories came flooding back to me. I promised myself I would revisit this recipe, and here it is.

Add the rest of the onion and hot pepper. Throw in the black pepper and keep stirring so nothing sticks or burns. Allow this to cook for about 6 minutes (or until the cabbage is almost tender) then add the can of corned beef. Break up the beef and stirring, cook for another 4 minutes or so.

Serve on a steaming bed of brown rice with a couple slices of avocado, with roti or fry bake, on buns like a Sloppy Joe or as a side dish. For a light snack, you can also pile bite-sized amounts on crackers.

Money's Worth: Please don't settle for the cheap canned corned beef. That stuff usually has a very mushy texture, is loaded with salt and has a lot of fat.

Name Your Amount: The amount of cabbage you use is entirely up to you, but two cups is a good starting point. When we all lived at home, there were six of us eating from one can of corned beef, so a lot more cabbage was added. Surprisingly, it still tasted the same.

Hold The Salt: I don't add any salt to this recipe because all canned corned beef comes packaged with a ton of salt and too much of anything is never good.

You'll Need...

- 2 cups cabbage
- 1 onion
- 1 teaspoon vegetable oil
- 1/2 scotch bonnet pepper, diced
- Dash black pepper
- 1 can corned beef

Start by shredding the cabbage then peel and dice the onion. In a pan, heat the oil on medium, add half of the diced onion and allow to cook until it is soft and translucent. Add the shredded cabbage. Keep the heat at medium and don't cover the pan or risk the entire dish going soggy from the liquid that the cabbage will release.

Because mom's mantra was, 'Eat what is cooked or starve', I grew up on fish, crab and just about all the seafood that was caught in the oceans surrounding the islands. I fondly remember my first experience with oyster cocktails at as early as five-years-old. Fresh oysters mixed in a spicy, tomato-based sauce, spiced with pepper sauce made from scotch bonnet peppers, was delectable. I couldn't even spell the word 'aphrodisiac', nor did I know the meaning, but I was chipping around town like Don Juan."

What would Sunday lunch—the biggest meal of the week on the islands—be without a serving of Callaloo, Stew Chicken, Macaroni Pie, rice and fried plantain? The main ingredient in the Callaloo dish is the baby leaves of the dasheen plant. In North America, however, finding dasheen leaves proves challenging. Instead, I use baby spinach.

You'll Need...

- **2 cans (400 ml) coconut milk**
- **Water (see step 1 for amount)**
- **2 lbs baby spinach**
- **1/2 onion, sliced**
- **6 cloves garlic**
- **1 lb okra**
- **1 cup pumpkin, diced**
- **1 teaspoon salt**
- **1/4 teaspoon black pepper**
- **3 sprigs thyme**
- **1 green scotch bonnet pepper**
- **2 crabs, each split into 2 pieces**
- **1/2 tablespoon green seasoning**
- **1 teaspoon Caribbean salted butter (optional)**
- **2 pimento peppers**

Heat a deep pot over medium and pour in coconut milk. Using one of the cans, add 2 cans of water so you have 4 cans of liquid in the pot. While it comes to a boil, wash spinach and start adding to the pot. It will seem like the spinach will not fit but as it wilts in the hot liquid, you'll have tons of room.

Wash and trim the okra by removing stems then slice each one into 1-inch pieces. Add sliced onions, garlic, okra, pumpkin, salt, black pepper, thyme and scotch bonnet pepper to the pot. Leave the scotch bonnet pepper whole, as you want the flavour rather than the raw heat. Cover pot, turn heat to gentle simmer and, stirring every 15 minutes or so, allow to cook for about 1 hour or until everything is tender and starts to break down. When stirring, check to ensure that

nothing is sticking to the bottom of the pot, which is an indication that your heat is too high.

45 minutes into the simmering process, season your crabs with green seasoning and allow them to marinate for 15 minutes before adding to the pot. After you've added the seasoned crab, allow the Callaloo to cook for another 15 minutes.

Remove the scotch bonnet pepper and crab from the pot but do not discard the crab. Using a whisk or handheld immersion blender, break down everything. If you are using a handheld blender, pulse a few times and do not use a continuous action or it will make the Callaloo frothy and can harm the finished product. If you're using a whisk, simply whisk until you get a soup-like consistency. Once you have a smooth texture, add the crab back to the pot. If using, add the Caribbean salted butter, stir and turn off heat.

Keep It Real: Crab meat or imitation crab will not give this dish the true savoury profile that crab still in its shell does.

Authenticity: Caribbean salted butter (a.k.a. Golden Ray brand) is uniquely different than traditional butter. It has a wonderful Creole flavour, which adds a distinct twist to the finished product. This butter can be found at West Indian and some Asian supermarkets.

Tools: If you have a wooden swizzle stick, use that during the breakdown step.

Vintage Trinbagonian Fish Broth

I inherited a love of Fish Broth (fish soup) from my Uncle B. After a weekend of partying, he'd usually make this soup because he claimed it's the best remedy for a hangover. As his sidekick in the kitchen, I'd be very involved in the preparation. Though it's been years since I last had this soup, I'd have to say that I did his recipe justice. One sip and I am taken back to the age of six or seven.

Bring to a boil, cover and reduce to a simmer for about 15 minutes.

Add the fish, butter and cilantro. After you've added the fish pieces, try not to over-stir or you risk breaking apart the fish. Cook for another 10-15 minutes on low heat. In the last 7 minutes, add the macaroni, if you wish.

You have a couple options with the finished dish. You can squeeze the lime juice directly into the pot or you can slice the lime and allow your guests to squeeze into their individual soup bowls. You can also top with chopped cilantro and additional hot sauce.

You'll Need...

- 1 fish (about 1 1/2 lbs), cuts into pieces
- Juice of half a lemon (to clean fish)
- 1 teaspoon green seasoning
- 1/2 teaspoon salt
- 1 tomato
- 2 potatoes
- 1 carrot
- 2 baby bok choy (pak choi)
- 1 onion
- 3 cloves garlic
- 1 scallion
- 1 rib celery
- 5 small okra
- 3 green cooking bananas, peeled
- 1/4 scotch bonnet pepper
- 1 tablespoon oil
- 4 cups fish stock
- 2 cups water
- 1 teaspoon Worcestershire sauce
- 1 tablespoon Caribbean salted butter
- 3 tablespoons cilantro, chopped
- Macaroni (your desired amount)
- 1 lime

Cut the fish into serving size pieces, clean according to the directions in the "Lime, Lemon or Vinegar!" section of the book. Season with green seasoning, salt and tomato. Set aside.

Chop and dice all the vegetables, including the potatoes, carrot, bok choy, onion, garlic, scallion, celery, okra, green bananas and hot pepper.

In a soup pot, add the oil and heat on medium-high. Drop in the onion and garlic, cooking for a few minutes before adding the rest of the prepped vegetables. Pour in 4 cups of fish stock, 2 cups of water and Worcestershire sauce.

Personalize: Though macaroni is an integral part of this dish, I don't have much of a pallet for pasta, so I don't include it in my preparation.

Choose Your Fish: I use sea bass, since this dish is usually made with "cheap" fish. The problem with using such a fish is that you will encounter many tiny bones, so be careful when eating. My suggestion would be to get any cheap fillet of ocean fish.

Authenticity: Caribbean salted butter (a.k.a. the Golden Ray brand) is uniquely different from traditional butter. It has a wonderful Creole flavour, which adds a distinct twist to the finished product. This butter can be found at West Indian and some Asian supermarkets.

A Dash Of Something Extra: For a new layer of flavour, add a couple drops of Angostura bitters near the end of the cooking process.

At no time was Shrimp Bisque cooked in my home when I was growing up. It would not be considered a traditional soup, as it was too fancy and light compared to the thick and hearty soups my mom would make! However, with the changing landscape of Caribbean cuisine, it's quite common to find this wonderful spicy seafood soup served at restaurants that cater to tourists and expats.

You'll Need...

- 1 lb shrimp (with heads and shells)
- Juice of 1 lime (to clean shrimp)
- 5 tablespoons butter
- 3 cups water
- 1/3 cup celery
- 2 scallions
- 1/4 scotch bonnet pepper
- 1/4 cup all-purpose flour
- 2 cups tomato soup
- 1/4 teaspoon curry powder
- Pinch each salt and black pepper
- 1/2 cup coconut milk

Remove shell and heads. Set aside but don't discard, as you will use them in the stock. Devein shrimp then wash clean according to the directions in the "Lime, Lemon or Vinegar!" section of the book.

Turn stove to medium heat, melt 2 tablespoons of butter in a deep pan, and add just shells and heads. Cook for about three minutes or until you notice them turn a sort of pink-orange colour. Add the water, bring to a boil and reduce to a gentle simmer. Allow it to simmer for 20 minutes.

In the meantime, cut each shrimp in half lengthwise then cut each strip in two pieces, so each shrimp gives you four pieces. Also, dice the celery, scallions and scotch bonnet pepper.

In another saucepan, on medium heat, melt the remaining butter, and add the celery, scallions and scotch bonnet pepper. Lower the heat a bit and allow that to gently cook

for 4-5 minutes then add the flour to the pot, whisking constantly or it will burn. The idea is to cook the flour and create a roux base for the bisque. The heat should be at minimum and it should cook for at least 5 minutes or you'll have a raw flour taste.

To the saucepan with the roux base, whisking as you go, add the tomato soup. Then, strain in the shrimp stock you made. It is important to add the tomato soup before the hot stock or you risk getting lumps. Once assembled, bring it to a simmer before adding the curry powder, salt and black pepper, and coconut milk. Stir, cover and simmer on low for 15 minutes.

After 15 minutes, it's time to add the pieces of raw shrimp. Since shrimp cooks

very fast, allow it to cook only for 1 minute and then turn off the stove. The residual heat will fully cook the shrimp. Check for salt and adjust accordingly.

Keep It Intact: I use shrimp with both the shell and head, as those parts are needed for making the bisque's stock. If you purchased already peeled and deveined shrimp, you may have to use a seafood stock for additional flavour.

Quality: Try to get a good tomato soup, not the canned stuff. I find the canned version has a sort of metallic taste, which will not compliment your bisque.

Stewed Pumpkin with Shrimp

Like okra, pumpkin is one of those foods I'm just starting to really appreciate. Pumpkin is heavily used throughout the Caribbean to add extra body to stews, soups, and how could I not mention the classic Pumpkin Rice? Even desserts like Cassava Pone can contain pumpkin. However, ever since my mom made Stewed Pumpkin with Shrimp for me, it's at the top of my list.

You'll Need...

- 1 cup shrimp
- Juice of 1/2 lemon (to clean shrimp)
- 1/4 teaspoon black pepper
- 1 teaspoon green seasoning
- 4 cups pumpkin, cut into 1-inch pieces
- 1 medium onion
- 3 cloves garlic
- 1/2 scotch bonnet pepper
- 1 tablespoon extra virgin olive oil
- 1/2 teaspoon salt
- 3/4 teaspoon golden brown sugar

Devein and clean shrimp according to the directions in the "Lime, Lemon or Vinegar!" section of the book. Add the black pepper and green seasoning, and stir well. As you get ready to cook, let that marinate. There's no need to marinate too long or the green seasoning will start cooking the shrimp.

Using a sharp knife or potato peeler, peel then cube and wash your pumpkin. As it's thick and waxy, the skin may be a bit tough so be careful. Chop the onion and scotch bonnet pepper, and crush or chop the garlic into thin slices.

Heat the oil on medium and add the seasoned shrimp. Stir quickly, as you want to cook the shrimp half way through and create a flavour base at the same time. After 2 minutes, remove the shrimp and place into the same bowl in which it was marinated.

Add the onion and garlic to the pan, and cook for 3 minutes on low heat then add

the slices of scotch bonnet pepper and give everything a good stir. After draining the cubed pumpkin, add it as well. Top with the salt, stir well and place the lid on the pot. After 2-3 minutes, you'll start to hear a sort of sizzle. That's the pumpkin releasing its own juices as it starts to boil. Give the contents of the pot another stir, turn the heat to low and let it simmer for about 25 minutes. Stir every 4-5 minutes.

After 25 minutes, the pumpkin should start to melt away and you'll notice a lot of liquid in the pot. Remove the lid and turn up the heat to start burning off that liquid, as an ideal Stewed Pumpkin with Shrimp has a drier finish. After most of the liquid is gone (about 4-5 minutes), add the semi-cooked

shrimp back to the pot. Stir in the brown sugar and continue cooking for another 4 minutes to burn off any remaining liquid.

Taste for salt and adjust accordingly. For a relatively smooth finish, you can use the back of your cooking spoon to crush any remaining chunks of pumpkin. If you like it a bit chunky, do nothing.

Authenticity: I use the type of pumpkin that's common in the Caribbean. It may be called calabaza, Caribbean pumpkin, Cuban squash or West Indian pumpkin. It can be found at West Indian and Latin grocery stores.

I've always had a weakness for curry potato, especially with hot Sada Roti (see the recipe on page 144) on the side to sop up the lovely gravy. Likewise, I've never been known to back away for a good dose of curry shrimp, which should be a bit spicy and not overcooked. So, many moons ago when my mom introduced me to this combination dish, I was in my own Shangri-La.

Curry Potato with Shrimp is excellent with rice, roti or bread and I assure you that even your kids will love it. If not, send me their names and I'll let Santa know they were bad this year.

You'll Need...

- 1/2 lb shrimp
- Juice of 1 lime (to clean shrimp)
- 1 teaspoon green seasoning
- 1 medium onion
- 4 cloves garlic
- 1/2 scotch bonnet pepper
- 4 medium potatoes
- 1 tablespoon vegetable oil
- 1 tablespoon curry powder
- 1/4 cup water
- 1/2 teaspoon amchar masala
- 1/2 teaspoon salt
- 1 1/2 cups water
- 2 tablespoons parsley

Peel and devein the shrimp then clean according to the directions in the "Lime, Lemon or Vinegar!" section of the book. Rinse with cool water and drain. Add the green seasoning to the shrimp and give it a good stir. Allow that to marinate for about 10 minutes.

Peel and chop the onion, garlic and scotch bonnet pepper. Then peel, wash and cube the potatoes.

In a deep saucepan, on medium, heat the vegetable oil then add the garlic and onion. Reduce your heat to low and allow this to cook for 3 minutes or until it's nice and soft. You'll also get that lovely scent of cooked onion and garlic. Add the sliced scotch bonnet pepper and curry powder and,

with your heat still on low, allow the curry powder to toast for 2-3 minutes.

Add about 1/4 cup of water and deglaze the pan (this means simply scraping the bottom of the pan as liquid is added). In the first step, you toasted the curry and now you're cooking it, so you don't get a raw curry aftertaste. Bring this to a boil and allow it to gently simmer for 4-5 minutes, then turn up the heat and burn off all the liquid. The curry paste will go a bit grainy and clump to the cooked onion, garlic and scotch bonnet pepper.

Add the diced potato, give it a good stir then add the amchar masala and salt, and pour in the 1 1/2 cups water. Reduce your heat to a simmer and let it cook, with the lid on, for about 20 minutes or until the potato becomes tender and liquid starts to thicken.

After 20 minutes, add the seasoned shrimp to the pot. Let it cook for 1 minute then check for salt (adjust accordingly). If you find the gravy is too thin, using the back of your spoon, crush a few pieces of potato to thicken it. Keep in mind that as this Curry Potato with Shrimp cools, it will naturally thicken up.

Turn off the stove, top with the chopped parsley and allow the residual heat to finish cooking the shrimp.

Size Matters: Use small shrimp for best results. They are more "sweet", as we say in the Caribbean.

Substitute: If you can't source amchar masala, use 1/4 teaspoon ground cumin.

Quick Shrimp Stir-Fry

When I was young, my dad would take my brother and I to see kung fu movies in the south Trinidad town of San Fernando. Besides being excited about the fighting scenes, which we'd try to emulate on each other when we got home, the Saturday outings also meant grabbing food from some of the popular Chinese restaurants on Mucurapo Street.

As I mentioned before, Chinese labourers, who settled in the region over one hundred years ago, heavily influenced the cuisine of many of the Caribbean islands.

kitchen should already have a wicked aroma. Add all the vegetables to the pan, stirring as you add to allow everything to hit the bottom of the wok and start cooking. Let that cook for 3-4 minutes then add the shrimp back with the addition of fresh ground white pepper, if using.

Pour your prepared sauce mixture over the vegetables and stir well. Basically, you're heating the sauce and allowing it to coat all those wonderful vegetables. I like my stir-fry with a bit of a crunch, so I don't cook it more than 2-3 minutes after I add the sauce. When you remove the stir-fry from the heat, remember to check for salt then serve immediately.

You'll Need...

- 1/2 lb shrimp
- Juice of 1 lime (to clean shrimp)
- 1 clove garlic, minced
- 1/2 teaspoon ginger, minced
- 1 large onion
- 1 carrot
- 1 cabbage
- 1 christophene ("chocho" to my Jamaican friends)
- 1 1/2 cups snow peas
- 1 1/2 cups orange, green and red bell pepper
- 1 1/2 cups mushrooms
- 1 1/2 cups baby bok choy (pak choi)
- 3 tablespoons dark soy sauce
- 1 tablespoon oyster sauce
- 1 tablespoon hoisin sauce
- 1 teaspoon sesame oil
- 1 teaspoon hot sauce (optional)
- Freshly ground white pepper (optional)
- 3 tablespoons vegetable oil, divided

Peel and devein shrimp, then clean according to the directions in the "Lime, Lemon or Vinegar!" section of the book. Also peel and chop the vegetables, trying to keep them similar in size so they cook uniformly.

In a small bowl, mix the soy, oyster and hoisin sauces as well as the sesame oil and hot sauce.

In a wok or pan, on medium-high, heat 1 tablespoon of the vegetable oil then add the shrimp. Cook for a couple minutes then remove from pan and set aside. Add the additional 2 tablespoons of oil to the pan, and toss in the onion, garlic and ginger. Let that cook until the onion is soft (about 2-3 minutes). The entire

Prep Is Key: It's very important that you have everything, including the sauce mixture, prepped before you get started.

Hold The Salt: As you are using soy sauce, you don't have to add any additional salt. However, it is entirely up to you since everyone's love for salt is different.

It's Your Choice: You can decide what vegetables you add and how much of each you actually use.

Substitute: If shrimp is not your thing, you can certainly use chicken or go vegetarian. I've also seen some vegetarian/simulated flavour oyster and hoisin sauces at my local Asian grocery store.

Serve It Up: The longer this stir-fry stays in the pan or if you cover it when it's done, it will continue cooking and go soggy.

Fry Okra With Shrimp

Over the years, my appreciation for okra has heightened. It is an often overlooked yet delicious addition that can enhance the taste of many meals. So, when a friend with Guyanese roots passed this recipe onto me, I can't tell you how excited I was to give it a try. Years later, I can safely says it is one of my favourite okra dishes. I hope I do it justice.

You'll Need...

- 1 lb okra
- 2 scallions
- 1 medium onion
- 3 cloves garlic
- 1/4 scotch bonnet pepper
- 2-3 tablespoons celery leaves
- 1 lb shrimp
- Juice of 1 lime (to clean shrimp)
- 3 tablespoons vegetable oil
- 1/4 teaspoon black pepper
- 1/2 teaspoon salt

Prepare okra according to the directions in the "Goodbye Slimy Okra Texture" section of the book.

Chop the scallions, onion, garlic, scotch bonnet pepper and celery leaves.

Clean shrimp according to the directions in the "Lime, Lemon or Vinegar!" section of the book. If they are large, cut your cleaned and deveined shrimp into small pieces.

On low, in a heavy pan, heat vegetable oil then add the chopped ingredients as well as the black pepper. Cook for a couple minutes to really bring out the flavours then add the shrimp. Turn your heat to medium and cook for 2-3 minutes.

You now have two options. First, to avoid overcooking, you can remove the shrimp and set it aside then add back to the pan during the final 2 minutes of cooking. Secondly, you can keep the shrimp in the pan and add the okra. Either way, keep stirring because the okra can start to stick to the bottom of the pan, which is why you started off with so much oil.

Allow the okra and shrimp to cook for about 7-10 minutes, uncovered. You will see the edges of the okra start to turn slightly brown, which, in my humble opinion, is the best part of this dish. At this point, remember to re-add the cooked shrimp if you removed it earlier. Add the salt, give it a good stir and you're done.

Size Matters: Smaller shrimp tend to have a "sweeter" flavour, as we say in the Caribbean. I would recommend using small ones if you have access to them.

Jamaican-Inspired Pepper Shrimp

The home of Pepper Shrimp in Jamaica is Middle Quarters (Saint Elizabeth Parish). And if you've ever had the pleasure of visiting the island, you may have been approached by ladies selling Pepper Shrimp in little plastic bags. Though their method of preparing this snack is a bit different than mine, I assure you that this recipe will rival any found on the island.

Pepper Shrimp is a wonderfully spicy snack that's great when having drinks with friends or, as in my case, reminiscing about a memorable Jamaican vacation. When you visit Jamaica, remember to check out the ladies in Middle Quarters and tell them Chris from CaribbeanPot.com said to find them for the best Pepper Shrimp on the island.

notice the colour will turn a bright sort of orange as the shrimp cooks. At this point, if you'd like, you can place a lid on the pot for about a minute or two. After 3 minutes, add the lemon juice. This bit of liquid will help release some of the garlic and pepper, which by now is probably sticking to the bottom of the pan. The shrimp will also let out its juices, so there's no need for any other liquid. It should take about 7 minutes for the shrimp to be cook. Try not to overcook or you'll risk the shrimp going rubbery.

Top with the chopped parsley, give it a final stir and serve.

You'll Need...

- 1 lb shrimp (30 /40)
- 1 Juice of 1 lime (to clean shrimp)
- 4 cloves garlic
- 1 scotch bonnet pepper
- 3/4 teaspoon salt
- 1 tablespoon paprika
- 2 tablespoons lemon juice
- 2 tablespoons parsley

Working with whole shrimp (in its shell with head still attached), use kitchen scissors to trim off legs and antennae. Clean freshly trimmed shrimp according to the directions in the "Lime, Lemon or Vinegar!" section of the book.

Finely dice the garlic and pepper, as you don't want to bite into big pieces of either when eating. To control the heat, you can certainly remove the seeds from the pepper and discard. The seeds and white membrane surrounding them is where most of the heat resides.

Heat a pan on medium-high (no oil is necessary, as you'll be sort of scalding the shrimp). Add the shrimp and give it a good stir then add the garlic, pepper, salt and paprika and stir well to coat everything. Stirring continuously, you'll

Throw Away Tradition: Traditionally, parsley and paprika are not used in this dish. However, I love the brightness of parsley and the sort of smoky undertones of the paprika. In true Jamaican fashion, a dash of pimento powder would be a good inclusion as well.

Keep It Intact: Cooking the entire shrimp is the way it's traditionally done in Jamaica. Plus, I love the sweetness of the shrimp when it's cooked this way. The shrimp steams in its own shell and this process seems to heighten the rich flavours.

Safety First: When handling the shrimp and/or hot pepper, you may want to wear gloves. Both can cause irritation to sensitive skin.

Whenever my family visits the Caribbean, we make it our mission to search out restaurants with Coconut Shrimp on the menu. Nothing beats freshly caught shrimp and flakes of coconut that have been grated on-site. Here's a quick Coconut Shrimp with Spicy Mango Dipping Sauce recipe. You can whip it up the next time you have friends over or when you're attending a company potluck and want to contribute something "island-like".

You'll Need...

- 1 lb shrimp (with tails attached)
- Juice 1 of lime (to clean shrimp)
- 2 eggs
- 1/2 teaspoon salt
- 1/4 scotch bonnet pepper, finely diced
- 3 tablespoons all-purpose flour
- 1 1/4 cups sweetened coconut flakes
- 3-4 cups vegetable oil

Start by preparing the shrimp. If your shrimp is already deveined, all you have to do is remove the shell-like outer layer. Keep the tail for appearance and handling. Then, using a paring knife, cut a deep slit along the same line where it was deveined (around the natural curve) to "butterfly" the shrimp. The idea is to cut deep but not all the way through. Clean shrimp according to the directions in the "Lime, Lemon or Vinegar!" section of the book.

In a bowl, place the eggs, salt, pepper and flour then give it a good whisk. You should have a smooth, but runny batter.

Set up an assembly line with the cleaned shrimp, coconut flakes (on a plate) and batter. Also, line a chopping board or a cookie sheet with parchment paper. Holding each shrimp by the tail, dip them, one at a time, in the batter. Coat evenly and place onto the coconut flakes (you may need to pat the flakes on a bit to stick properly). Place each coated shrimp onto the parchment-lined chopping board or cookie sheet. Repeat until all the

shrimp is coated. The idea is to batter all the shrimp before you start, as they will cook very fast and you may not be quick enough when frying.

When the oil is heated to about 375 F, start adding about 5-6 shrimp at a time. Do not overcrowd the pan. They will start curling in and changing colour as they cook. You want the coconut coating to turn a golden-brown. Cook for 1-2 minutes on each side then take out and place on paper towels to drain excess oil.

This Coconut Shrimp is best enjoyed freshly made. However, you can cover it with plastic wrap and store it in the fridge for about 4 hours. Then heat in a 350 F-oven until crisp and hot, about 6 minutes.

The Spicy Mango Dipping Sauce to accompany this tasty Coconut Shrimp is very easy to make.

☞ **Find the Spicy Mango Dipping Sauce recipe on youtube.com/caribbeanpot**

Jamaican-Style Escovitch Fish

This Jamaican-Style Escovitch Fish takes me back 21 years when, as teenagers, my friends and I would head to Toronto to shop for records for our aspiring DJ business. Remember 45's and 33's? Those trips usually led us to the Jamaican community on Eglinton Avenue in the city's west end. In this area, not only were there many record stores that sold the latest dancehall tracks from Jamaica, but also quite a few restaurants where we would get our Curry Goat, Rice and Peas, and this lovely Escovitch Fish.

Back in those days, we never had enough money for each of us to get a fish, so it usually meant sharing a plate. The little bit of extra money we saved went towards getting the latest Shabba Ranks records. Good times, for sure! My good friend still does the DJ thing (he's very passionate about music) and has turned it into a huge business.

You'll Need...

- 1 red snapper (about 2 lbs)
- 1 lime (to clean fish)
- 1 scallion
- 3 sprigs thyme
- 1/4 teaspoon salt
- 1/4 teaspoon black pepper
- About 1 cup vegetable oil

Sauce...
- 3/4 cup vinegar
- 1/4 teaspoon allspice
- 1 large onion
- 1 carrot
- 1 cup green bell pepper (or different colours if you like)
- 1 scotch bonnet pepper
- Pinch salt
- 1/2 teaspoon white sugar

Trim fish, then clean according to the directions in the "Lime, Lemon or Vinegar!" section of the book. Using a sharp knife, cut a couple of slits across both side of the fish's belly. This will allow for faster cooking and help the salt, black pepper and escovitch sauce to infuse the fish.

Using the back of your knife, hit the scallion to bruise it and release its flavour. Fold the scallion and tuck it into the cavity of the fish. Also tuck in the sprigs of thyme. You want to perfume the fish from the inside out. Lastly, rub the salt and black pepper onto both sides of the fish in preparation for frying.

In a pan, heat the vegetable oil on medium then gently add the seasoned fish. Allow it fry for 4-5 minutes on each side or until you have a nice golden colour and crisp outside. Remove the fish from the pan and place on paper towels to soak up excess oil.

While the fish is resting, make the escovitch sauce. Julienne the carrot and bell pepper, chop the onion, and slice scotch bonnet pepper. Add all ingredients for the sauce to a saucepan, place on medium heat and bring to a gentle simmer for 3-5 minutes or until the onion and bell pepper become tender.

Place the fried snapper on a platter and pour the escovitch sauce over it. Enjoy!

Substitute: Typically, pimento berries are used but ground allspice is pretty much the same thing. Although it may sound strange, the addition of sugar balances the escovitch sauce so, give it a try.

Storage: You can store any remaining escovitch sauce in an airtight container in the fridge for a couple of weeks.

This Caribbean-Inspired Grilled Red Snapper will cause your taste buds to go into a state of frenzy when they're hit with bite after bite of exciting flavour. After growing up on fried, curried and stewed fish, the past few years have seen me adopt new and exciting ways to prepare seafood. This is certainly one of them.

You'll Need...

- 1 red (1-2 lbs) snapper
- Juice of 1 lemon (to clean fish)
- 1/2 scotch bonnet pepper
- 1 pimento pepper
- 1 scallion
- 4 sprigs thyme
- 3 sprigs dill (optional)
- 1/4 teaspoon black pepper
- 1/4 teaspoon salt
- 2 slices lemon
- 2 tablespoons coconut milk
- Banana leaf, for wrapping the fish

Scale, trim and clean fish according to the directions in the "Lime, Lemon or Vinegar!" section of the book. Using a sharp knife, make shallow cuts (every inch or so) across the thick part of the fish's belly then set aside. Chop the scotch bonnet and pimento peppers and, using the back of your knife, tap the scallion to bruise it and release its flavours.

Cut open the bottom cavity (belly) of the fish. Fold the scallion and tuck into the belly then do the same with peppers, thyme and dill.

Place stuffed fish on the banana leaf and season both sides with black pepper and salt, using your fingers to get some into the small cuts. Place the 2 slices of lemon on top of the fish and cover with coconut milk.

Fold banana leaf over the fish (try to tuck it in to secure) to form a parcel. Seal the ends as well.

Place on a hot 375 F grill. I use a grill with three burners, so I leave the far-left burner on high and the 2 burners directly below the fish on medium-low. Close the BBQ's lid and cook, depending on how thick the fish is, for about 12-15 minutes. Flip and cook for the same amount of time on the other side. If you find your flame is burning the banana leaves, turn the heat to low. It's normal for the banana leaves to be slightly charred, so don't panic!

Using a pair of scissors (be careful as there may be steam), cut open the parcel and enjoy. Remember, this is a whole fish, so there will be bones.

Look For It: Pimento peppers can be found in West Indian and Latin grocery stores.

Substitute: If you can't source banana leaf, use tin foil or parchment paper.

Fried Seasoned Red Snapper

As kids, the only way my mom could get my siblings and I to eat fish was to pan fry kingfish and serve it with ketchup and some pepper sauce. To get my daughters to like fish—something most North American kids hate with a passion—my mom purposely cooked the same meal when she visited. It really made them appreciate the deliciousness that is fish.

Seasoned to perfection and marinated for a couple hours, this fish is then dusted in flour and pan-fried. This recipe traditionally uses kingfish but can be adapted for any fish you like. These days, I usually use small red snappers, as kingfish is very pricey.

You'll Need...

- 2 lbs red snapper
- Juice of 1 lemon (to clean fish)
- 1/2 teaspoon salt
- 1/4 teaspoon black pepper
- 1/4 onion, finely diced
- 1/2 teaspoon pepper sauce
- 1/4 teaspoon curry powder
- 1 teaspoon green seasoning
- 2 cloves garlic, crushed
- 1/2 cup all-purpose flour
- Vegetable oil (for frying)

Clean the fish according to the directions in the "Lime, Lemon or Vinegar!" section of the book. Make shallow cut across the belly of the fish so the marinade can infuse it. Depending on the fish's size, two cuts may be necessary.

Place the fish in a bowl then cover it with everything except the flour and oil. Massage the mixture into the belly cavity and cuts you made. Cover and allow it to marinate in the fridge for at least 1 hour.

In a deep pan, on medium, heat about 2-3 cups of oil. While it heats, set up a station with a plate of flour and a plate lined with paper towels to drain the excess oil after frying.

Dredge the fish in the flour. Don't worry about shaking off the marinade because it will be delightful when cooked with the fish. Gently place each fish into the hot oil, careful not to crowd the pan. The idea is to cook the fish on each side for about 4-6 minutes (depending on the thickness of the fish you use and how crisp you like it).

Once each fish is fried, place it on the paper towels to drain then serve warm. If you're reheating these, I would recommend doing so in an oven rather than a microwave.

Kick It Up: You can use finely chopped scotch bonnet pepper or any hot sauce you like instead of pepper sauce.

Safety First: If you're using a whole fish, remember there will be bones that are a choking hazard. This recipe also works great with fish fillets (bones removed), which would be a good option if you plan on serving the dish to kids. You may ask why bother with anything but fillets? If you've ever had a whole fried fish, you'll know how tasty it can be.

Air It Out: When making this Fried Seasoned Red Snapper, be sure to open the windows in your kitchen and turn on the exhaust fan if you have one. The scent of fried fish will linger.

Curry Kingfish

A while back, when doing one of those online "20 Questions" questionnaires, I was asked, "What would be your last meal?" Without batting an eye, I answered, "My mom's Curry Kingfish". The rich curry sauce with thick slices of pre-fried kingfish is simply stunning. I could never truly duplicate her recipe but this one is pretty close.

You'll Need...

- 4 slices kingfish (about 1 1/2 lbs)
- Juice of 1 lemon (to clean fish)
- 1 onion
- 1 scallion
- 2 cloves garlic
- 1 tomato
- 1/2 scotch bonnet pepper
- 3 leaves shado beni
- 1/2 teaspoon salt
- 1/4 teaspoon black pepper
- 1/2 teaspoon amchar masala
- 2 tablespoons curry powder
- 1 tablespoon green seasoning
- 1/2 cup bell pepper (optional)
- 4 tablespoons all-purpose flour
- About 2 cups vegetable oil
- 1 cup of water

Clean fish according to the directions in the "Lime, Lemon or Vinegar!" section of the book. Chop the onion, scallion, garlic, tomato and scotch bonnet pepper. Give the shado beni a rough chop as well and set aside.

Place cleaned fish slices in a large bowl and season with salt, black pepper, amchar masala, 1/3 of the curry powder, green seasoning, 1/2 of the chopped onion, the chopped tomato, scallions, scotch bonnet pepper and bell pepper, if using. Marinate in the fridge for at least 1 hour.

When ready to cook, set up an assembly line of seasoned fish, a shallow plate with flour, a pan (on medium-high heat) with oil for frying and paper towels to drain. Shake off any extra marinade from the fish (do not discard the bowl with the marinade quite yet), dredge in flour and place in hot oil, being careful that it doesn't splatter and burn you. Fry on each side for 4 minutes, as not to overcook the fish. Set aside.

In a deep saucepan, heat 2 tablespoons of vegetable oil on medium-high then toss in the remaining half of the onion and garlic. Reduce your heat to low and let that cook gently for a couple of minutes. You should have a nice flavour base at this point, so toss in the remaining curry powder and stir well. It will start to go darker and grainy. Stir and allow to bloom for 3 minutes. Your kitchen should have that "wicked" aroma by now. Add the marinade in which you had your fish into the pan and give it a good stir before turning the heat to medium and bringing to a boil. Add 1 cup of water to the same bowl in which you marinated the fish and swish around to get any remaining marinade. Pour that water into the pan and bring to a boil.

Simmer 3-5 minutes to allow all those flavours to marry and make good things happen. Gently add the pieces of fish to the pan. Allow to simmer 5 minutes and, if you can, flip fish pieces without breaking apart. If not, spoon some of that curry sauce over the fish as it simmers. As the sauce thickens, the fish will be infused with all the wonderful flavours.

When you turn off the stove, top the fish with the chopped shado beni and place the lid on the pan for a few minutes before serving with rice, roti, ground provisions or on its own.

DIY Amchar Masala: To make your own amchar masala, in a dry frying pan, toast 4 tbsp coriander seeds, 1 tbsp cumin seeds, 2 tsp black peppercorns, 1 tsp whole fennel seeds, 1 tsp brown mustard seeds, 1 tsp fenugreek seeds. Grind in a coffee grinder or use a mortar and pestle.

My Take On Saltfish Buljol

In the Caribbean, saltfish is king. Used on its own or as a flavour enhancer, it's now found in many dishes up and down the islands. Gone are the days when saltfish was considered a poor man's meal and since the decline of the cod population in eastern Canada, it's actually become very expensive.

Though close to the real deal, this recipe is not how traditional Saltfish Buljol is made. My dad would tell us that his grandparents' Buljol was very simple. It consisted of shredded saltfish that was topped with hot oil, and sliced onions, hot peppers and tomato (if you were lucky enough to have those additions).

Heat the olive oil in a frying pan and just before it starts to smoke, drizzle it onto everything in the bowl. Mix thoroughly and serve with ground provisions, rice and dhal, stuffed into fry bake, on sandwiches or as a topping for crackers. If you add a bit more tomato, green and red bell peppers, and toss in some shredded cabbage, you'll have a great salad.

The World According To Saltfish: Saltfish and the dishes made from it are known by many different names. For example, in a few countries saltfish starts with a B: baccalà (Italy), bacalhau (Portugal), bacalao (Spain) and bakalar (Croatia). Meanwhile in France, it's morue; in Scandinavia, klippfisk/clipfish. And in Iceland, where it's closest to English, it's called saltfiskur.

Choose Your Saltfish: In this recipe, I use salted Alaska pollock, but you're free to use cod, hake or any other saltfish you may have available to you. I would also recommend that you get the boneless variety to avoid having to remove the tiny bones when preparing this dish.

Safety First: When handling the hot pepper, you may want to wear gloves. Peppers can cause irritation to sensitive skin.

You'll Need...

- 1/4 lb saltfish
- 1/4 cup green bell pepper, cubed
- 1/2 medium onion, very thinly sliced
- 1 medium tomato, cubed
- 1 scallion, thinly sliced
- 1 clove garlic, crushed
- Dash black pepper
- 4 tablespoons extra virgin olive oil

Prepare the saltfish according to the directions in the "One Pong (pound) of Saltfish and Come Straight Home" section of the book.

Flake or shred the prepared saltfish and squeeze dry. Add the sliced, diced and chopped bell pepper, onion, tomato, scallion and garlic to the bowl with the shredded saltfish. Give it a good dose of freshly cracked black pepper and mix.

Saltfish Stir-Fry

When you grow up in a home where saltfish rules, you're always looking for different ways to use this fine ingredient. So, here's my take on a classic island stir-fry. In writing the recipe, it occurred to me that I've never made it for my dad, who's a connoisseur of saltfish. I'll have to remedy that soon. According to him, every meal should contain saltfish.

- 1 cup carrots, julienned
- 1 1/2 cups bell pepper (any colour you like)
- 2 scallions, chopped
- 2 cups cabbage, thickly shredded
- Pinch black pepper
- 1 teaspoon dark soy sauce

Prepare the saltfish according to the directions in the "One Pong (pound) of Saltfish and Come Straight Home" section of the book.

On high, heat the oil in a wok or non-stick pan and add the flaked saltfish pieces. Toss around for 30 seconds then add the onion, ginger, thyme and scotch bonnet pepper. Cook for 1 minute then add all the vegetables. Stir and cook for about 2-3 minutes.

Add the black pepper and soy sauce, mix well and cook for another 1-2 minutes. The salt from the soy sauce and the remaining salt in the fish will be enough to season this dish.

To Kick It Up (Or Not): The scotch bonnet pepper is optional if you're worried about any heat, but it's a nice addition.

Colour Me Red, Yellow or Green: To give the dish a bright and attractive appearance, try to use a combination of different coloured bell peppers.

You'll Need...

- 3/4 cup flaked saltfish
- 2 tablespoons vegetable oil
- 1 medium onion, sliced
- 1/4 teaspoon ginger, grated
- 1 teaspoon fresh thyme, finely chopped
- 1/4 scotch bonnet pepper, finely chopped (optional)

The Ultimate Ackee and Saltfish

A few years ago, when visiting my friend Dino's mom at her home in Portmore, Jamaica, my family and I were lucky to have her cook a traditional breakfast. I have to confess that it was my first experience with Ackee and Saltfish, but I quickly fell in love with Jamaica's national dish. That lovely morning, we also had boiled green cooking banana, yam, dumplings and some of the best hard dough bread I've ever had. We washed it all down with a piping hot cup of Milo, sweetened with my favourite condensed milk.

In this recipe, I use canned ackee and though I assure you that it's very delicious, it cannot compare to the fresh ackee that was prepared for us in Jamaica. Nonetheless, this recipe is outstanding.

In a large saucepan, heat the oil on medium. Add garlic, onions and scotch bonnet pepper, and cook until the onion softens. Add the bell pepper, scallion, black pepper and thyme, and allow this to cook for a couple minutes. Add the pieces of saltfish and cook for another 3-5 minutes. To prevent the tomato from becoming too mushy, add and let it warm through only for 1-2 minutes. Stir, so all the ingredients get a chance to bask in this explosion of spectacular flavour.

It's time to introduce the star of the show. Here's the thing about canned ackee: It's very fragile. After you open the can, pour everything into a strainer and run cold water over it to remove the liquid it's been packed in. After it drains, add the ackee to the saucepan with everything else. But instead of stirring with a spoon, use two forks and gently toss it with the other ingredients. The trick is to not break it apart or you'll end up with a huge pot of mush. Heat through for 1-2 minutes, letting the ackee absorb those wonderful layers of flavour you built.

You'll Need...

- 1/2 lb boneless, skinless saltfish
- 2 tablespoons olive oil
- 2 cloves garlic, thinly sliced
- 1 medium onion, sliced
- 1 scotch bonnet pepper (or habanero), de-seeded
- 1/4 medium bell pepper, sliced
- 2 scallions, chopped
- 1/4 teaspoon black pepper
- 2 sprigs thyme
- 1 medium tomato, cubed
- 1 can ackee (about 2 cups fresh, if available)

Prepare the saltfish according to directions in the "One Pong (pound) of Saltfish and Come Straight Home" section of the book. Break apart the fish into the size you like. I've seen people use a fork to shred the saltfish, but I like the texture of large flakes.

Oil Matters: I like using olive oil but you can use vegetable oil or butter, as I've seen some people do.

Hold The Salt: Since you're using saltfish, there's no need for any salt in this dish.

This Green Cooking Banana With Cabbage and Saltfish is a tribute to the wonderful people of St. Lucia. During my first trip to the island many moons ago, I was fortunate enough to have something very similar and I remember my hosts saying that it was their country's national dish. I never really confirmed this because I was too caught up enjoying the great food and general hospitality of St. Lucia.

tomato, and chop the garlic, thyme, parsley and scotch bonnet pepper.

In a deep saucepan, on medium, heat the vegetable oil. Add the prepped flaked saltfish and turn the heat to low. Let that cook for about 4 minutes, as you want to create a lovely flavour base.

Add the onion, garlic, scotch bonnet pepper, black pepper and thyme, and let cook for a further 3 minutes.

Toss in the shredded cabbage and give it a good stir. The green bananas should have cooled by now, so simply peel back and remove the skin. If you see any stringy fibres, remove those as well. Chop into 1-inch pieces, add to the saucepan and sprinkle with salt.

Turn the heat up to medium-low and make sure to mix everything well so the flavours coat the green bananas. After about 4 minutes (depending on how cooked you want the cabbage), toss in the diced tomato and parsley, and give it a stir. Cover the pot and turn off the heat, letting the residual heat finish the cooking process.

You'll Need...

- 2 lbs green cooking bananas
- 3/4 cup saltfish, shredded
- 2 cups cabbage
- 1 medium onion
- 1 medium tomato
- 2 cloves garlic
- 2 sprigs thyme
- 2 tablespoons parsley
- 1/4 scotch bonnet pepper
- 2 tablespoons vegetable oil
- Pinch black pepper
- 1/4 teaspoon salt

Trim the ends of the banana and discard. Then, using a sharp paring knife and following one of the natural ridges, make a shallow cut

(the thickness of the skin) down the length of the banana. Repeat until all are finished.

Place the trimmed bananas in a deep pot, cover with water and bring to a boil. Reduce to a rolling boil and let them cook for about 20 minutes. You'll notice two things: They will darken (even go black) and the slit that you made will open up. Drain and allow to cool so the bananas are easier to handle.

Prepare the saltfish according to the directions in the "One Pong (pound) of Saltfish and Come Straight Home" section of the book.

Shred the cabbage, dice the onion and

Hold The Salt: The fish will still retain some saltiness, so keep this in mind if adding salt to the dish.

Safety First: Coat your hands with vegetable oil or wear gloves, as the sap from the green bananas can stain or cause your hands to itch.

Steamed Fish with Cabbage and Okra

Here's a dish my family tore up during our Jamaican vacation. Like I mentioned before, growing up, I enjoyed fish curried, stewed and in fish broth. So, this steamed fish was new to me—especially when I saw it being served with crackers and Bammy (cassava flat bread). At first, a fish that looked as if it was boiled, with no real colour to it, was not at all appealing. However, after the first bite, I could only think, "I've been missing out all these years." It's also great on its own.

You'll Need...

- 2 cups fish stock
  (or water or vegetable stock)
- 10 okra
- 1 large onion
- 1 1/2 cups cabbage
- 2 fish (about 1 lb each)
- 1 lime or lemon (to clean fish)
- 3 scallions
- 1 1/2 scotch bonnet peppers
- 6 sprigs thyme
- 1/2 teaspoon black pepper, divided
- 2 medium tomatoes
- 2 cloves garlic
- 1/4 teaspoon salt

Heat the stock or water in a fairly large pot and bring to simmer. Meanwhile, cut off stems and cut each okra in half, and chop the onion and cabbage. Add the okra, onion and cabbage to the simmering stock. Cover pan with a lid and allow to reduce, on low heat, for about 5-7 minutes.

Meanwhile, clean the fish according to the directions in the "Lime, Lemon or Vinegar!" section of the book.

Chop the scallions into halves. Keep the green ends (about 4-5 inches) and dice the remaining pieces. Finely chop the half of the scotch bonnet pepper. Rinse the thyme under cool water but keep it intact on the sprig. If your fish is not cut down the middle of the belly, do so. Take about 3 sprigs of thyme, 1/2 of the scallions (green parts), chopped scotch bonnet pepper and a dash

of black pepper, and stuff the cavity of each fish with it. Make a couple of shallow cuts across both sides of the fish. This will ensure the fish cooks faster and nicely absorbs all the flavours.

Add the chopped tomato, garlic, the rest of the black pepper, and the seasoned fish into the pot. You may need to make room, so the fish can sit as deeply as possible in the pot. Give the pot a shake and spoon some of that rich broth you created over each fish. Bring to a boil, place the whole scotch bonnet pepper on top then reduce the heat to a simmer and cover the pot with a lid. Let this cook for about 10 minutes. Remember to add the salt near the end of

the cooking process and taste to see if you need more. Be mindful of whether the fish stock you use has salt in it, because that will account for some of the salt in the overall dish. Also, remember to remove the whole scotch bonnet from the pot.

Authenticity: I've seen vinegar and some butter used in preparing this dish. However, I'm no fan of vinegar and we could all do without the fat from the butter.

Choose Your Fish: I opted for sea bass, but a more sturdy fish like red snapper will work just as well.

Growing up, I wasn't a huge fan of cassava. Even today, it's a last ground provision resort when I can't find dasheen, yam and/or eddoes. When I do cook with it, I try to infuse some flavour with saltfish and other ingredients because I find it bland. In this recipe, I use frozen cassava that you can get in the frozen food section at most grocery stores. However, it works just as well with fresh cassava—as long as you're up for peeling and cubing it.

Start by dicing and slicing the bell peppers, shallot, scallion and garlic. Set aside.

To cook the frozen cassava, follow the instructions on the package. It should take about 20 minutes.

Meanwhile, prepare the saltfish according to the directions in the "One Pong (pound) of Saltfish and Come Straight Home" section of the book. Using your fingers or a fork, shred the fish into bits.

By now, the cassava should be fully cooked. To ensure that it is, pierce it with a knife and if there's no resistance, it's ready. Drain the liquid out and set aside.

Add the oil and butter to a saucepan, and heat on medium. Once the oil and butter are heated, add the saltfish and cook for about 4-5 minutes. Add the shallots and garlic, and allow this to cook for a further 3 minutes, stirring often. Lastly, add the sliced peppers and scallions, and cook for about 3-5 minutes on medium-low heat.

Add the cooked cassava. Stir so everything gets coated with the wonderful flavours of the saltfish, shallots, garlic and peppers. Cook for about 3-5 minutes.

You'll Need...

- 1/2 scotch bonnet pepper (or habanero)
- 1/4 green bell pepper
- 1/4 red, yellow or orange bell pepper (optional)
- 1 shallot (or onion)
- 1 scallion
- 2 cloves garlic
- 1 package frozen cassava (about 1 lb)
- About 1/4 cup saltfish, shredded
- 2 tablespoons olive oil
- 1 tablespoon butter
- Freshly ground black pepper (to taste)

Choose Your Fish: There are three options for buying saltfish: bone in, boneless and bits. The choice is yours. I use the boneless variety.

Fried Okra with Saltfish

My mom always had okra in her small garden at the back of our home and it was my duty to pick it for making Callaloo on Sundays. I'd be out there doing my job before the morning sun came up—getting wet from the dew drops on the plant leaves and being careful not to brush against the plant too much or risk having itchy skin. Here, okra is fried with saltfish for a delightful meal.

Prepare the okra according to directions in the "Goodbye Slimy Okra Texture" section of the book.

Prepare the saltfish according to directions in the "One Pong (pound) of Saltfish and Come Straight Home" section of the book.

On medium, heat the oil in a non-stick pan and add the saltfish. Reduce to low heat and allow to cook for 4-6 minutes. As fish pieces start to crisp and edges go brown, add the sliced onion, scotch bonnet pepper, garlic and black pepper. Cook on medium heat for a couple minutes.

Add the now-dried okra into the pan and stir well. For okra with a crunch, allow to cook, uncovered, for 20 minutes. You can certainly cook for more or less time. Top with the diced tomato, give it a good stir and allow to cook for 2 minutes. Taste for salt in the last couple minutes of cooking and adjust accordingly.

Hold The Salt: The saltfish will still contain salt after you've re-hydrated it, so you may not need to add any to the dish. If you are adding salt, it's important to do so near the end of the cooking process, as it will cause moisture to develop and you don't want that.

Tools: Cooking okra in this manner uses a lot of oil, so use a non-stick pan to help cut back on the amount of oil.

You'll Need...

- 1 lb okra
- 1 cup boneless saltfish
- 4 tablespoons vegetable oil
- 1 medium onion, sliced

- 1/2 scotch bonnet pepper, sliced
- 3 cloves garlic, sliced
- 1/4 teaspoon black pepper
- 1 tomato (seeds and liquid removed), diced

Saltfish Accras

Many of you may know this delight as Cod Fish Fritters, Saltfish Fritters and/or Fish Cakes. It's very common for dishes to have different names depending on what island you call home. Basically, these recipes use the same ingredients but each island adds its own personal touches.

You'll Need...

- 1/2 lb boneless saltfish
- 1/4 teaspoon fresh thyme
- 2 shado beni leaves
- 2 tablespoons scallions
- 1/2 teaspoon parsley (optional)
- 2 cloves garlic
- 1 teaspoon scotch bonnet pepper
- 1 small onion
- Dash freshly ground black pepper
- 1 cup all-purpose flour
- 2 teaspoons baking powder
- Pinch sugar
- 1 egg
- 1/4 to 1/2 cup water
- About 3 cups vegetable oil

Prepare the saltfish according to directions in the "One Pong (pound) of Saltfish and Come Straight Home" section of the book. Prep the herbs, garlic, pepper and onion by finely chopping and dicing.

You can certainly shred the saltfish with your fingers, but the texture may be a bit chunky. The other option is to use a food processor or a mortar and pestle. For the latter, place the fish pieces in the mortar and giving them a good pounding with the aid of the pestle. Even though you're using boneless saltfish, keep an eye out for any bones that may have snuck in.

In a large bowl, stirring as you add each new ingredient, combine the black pepper, flour, baking powder, sugar, garlic, onion, pepper and all the herbs. Then add the shredded saltfish and the egg, stirring to combine. Lastly, start adding water while stirring. The goal is to get a thick batter.

Heat the vegetable oil on medium-high. Before you start adding heaping teaspoonfuls of batter to the pan, be sure to have a draining station set up with paper towels on which to place the finished Accras. Do not overcrowd the pan.

Cooking time should take a couple minutes on each side and you'll notice the Saltfish Accras will start to float as they cook. You want to achieve a perfect golden-brown colour. If you find that the Accras are going dark quickly, you may have to turn down the heat or risk having Accras that are raw in the middle.

Air It Out: Leave your kitchen window open or turn on the fan above your stove. The scent of boiling saltfish is not for everyone.

A Dash Of Something Extra: Use milk instead of water when making the dough.

Perfect Partner: This is an excellent party finger food or snack and it goes well with my Spicy Tamarind Dipping Sauce.

☞ **You can find the dipping sauce recipe at caribbeanpot.com/a-tantalizing-tamarind-sauce/**

Spicy Fish Balls

I don't recall if it was in Guyana or in Barbados that I first had something similar to these Spicy Fish Balls, but I do recall how tasty they were. I knew I'd have to come up with a recipe sooner or later, so here it is. With the use of panko bread crumbs and Parmesan cheese, you'll see how international this version of fish balls is.

mix all the ingredients in a large bowl.

Take about a teaspoonful of the mixture and roll in your hands to form a ball. Repeat until you've used all of the mixture. Toss in the flour to evenly coat the outside. This will help you achieve that lovely golden-brown colour when the Spicy Fish Balls are fried. Be sure to dust them all before you start frying, as they cook very fast. So they don't stick as they wait their turn in the hot oil, you can place the prepared fish balls on a parchment paper-lined cookie sheet.

On medium-high, heat the oil then gently add the balls and fry for 3-4 minutes. I love using my wok, as it maintains an even heat and the high sides prevent me from making a mess on the stove. Drain on paper towels and serve warm. Try pairing the fish balls with one of the spicy sauces from the "Sauces, Condiments & Marinades" section of this book.

You'll Need...

- 1 lb fresh cod fillets
- Juice of 1/2 lemon (to clean fish)
- 2 cloves garlic, crushed
- 3/4 cup Parmesan cheese, grated
- 1 tablespoon each parsley and thyme, chopped
- 2 eggs
- 3/4 cup panko bread crumbs
- 1/4 teaspoon each salt and black pepper
- 1/2 scotch bonnet pepper, finely diced
- 2-3 cups vegetable oil
- 1/2 cup all-purpose flour

Clean fish according to the directions in the "Lime, Lemon or Vinegar!" section of the book. If you're using frozen cod, give it a good squeeze, as there's usually a lot of water in it. Cut into chunks and place into a food processor. Give the fish a few pulses and remember to scrape down the sides of the processor, so you get an even consistency. Add all the other ingredients, except the flour and the vegetable oil, and pulse for 1-2 minutes until everything is well mixed. If you don't have a food processor, don't fret. Simply chop the codfish very finely and

Heat Control: The diced scotch bonnet will give this a wicked kick so feel free to cut back on it or leave it out if you're overly concerned about the heat, you chicken.

Pre-Prep And Safety First: Remember to pre-chop the herbs very finely and crush the garlic. The scotch bonnet pepper should also be very fine. Do remember to wear gloves when handling it.

I'll admit that I'm country to the bone and have a weakness for all types of ground provisions—in soups, steamed, boiled, mashed, scalloped or roasted. But I have a special attachment to yams. After moving to Canada, I also fell in love with Corned Beef and Potato Hash. So, the creative side of my brain figured it would be nice to have a Caribbean version. Here, saltfish is used as a flavour enhancer.

You'll Need...

- 2-3 cups yam
- 2 tablespoons saltfish, shredded
- 1/4 scotch bonnet pepper, de-seeded
- 1 medium onion
- 2 tablespoons coconut oil (or olive oil)
- Pinch black pepper
- 1 tablespoon parsley (to garnish)

Before you begin, put on gloves or coat your hands with some vegetable oil because the sticky residue from the yam may irritate your skin. Using a potato peeler or sharp paring knife, peel the yam as you would normally peel a potato. If there are any black spots or blemishes, remove with the knife. Cube the yam and, to prevent discolouration, set in cool water until you're ready to cook it.

Prepare the saltfish according to the directions in the "One Pong (pound) of Saltfish and Come Straight Home" section of the book.

Dice the scotch bonnet pepper and onion.

On medium, heat the coconut oil in a non-stick frying pan (or well-seasoned cast iron pan) then add the onion and cook for about 3-4 minutes. Add the black pepper, scotch bonnet pepper and shredded saltfish. Allow this to cook for about 3-4 minutes, so you release the lovely accent of the fish.

Drain the cubed yam and add to the pot. With your heat on medium-low, cover the pot so the yam sort of steam cooks, stirring every 4 minutes. The dish should be fully cooked in about 20 minutes, with the natural sugars in the cubed yam giving the pieces a lovely golden-brown hue around the edges. You can remove the lid during the last 4 minutes of cooking and test if it's fully cooked by piercing a piece of yam with a sharp knife. If there's no resistance, you're good to go after you garnish with the chopped parsley.

Authenticity: I use Caribbean-style yams for this recipe, not the sweet potatoes that are usually called "yams" in North American grocery stores. If you visit your local West Indian, Latin or Asian food store, I'm sure you'll find these yams. They may be called Jamaican or West Indian yams. Sweet potato is a good alternative for this recipe, but you may need to balance the natural sweetness of it.

Gourmet Canned Salmon

I'm not sure if this should be classified as a recipe, but I do know that among Caribbean people, it's affectionately known as "bache" or bachelor food. "Bache" usually refers to any meal that can be prepared in less than ten minutes.

When I was a kid, this was a normal part of Good Friday lunch. We had access to tons of fresh fish on islands, but somehow canned salmon still made its way onto our menu. It was either served on rice or with lovely ground provisions like yam, eddoes and dasheen. My dad used to top his with olive oil, something I only learned to appreciate as an adult.

You'll Need...

- 1 (231 g) can salmon (sockeye, pink or tea rose keta salmon)
- 1 medium tomato
- 1 scallion
- 1 shado beni leaf
- 1 clove garlic
- 1 medium onion
- 1 teaspoon ketchup
- 1/4 scotch bonnet pepper (optional)
- 1 sprig thyme
- Pinch salt
- Dash black pepper

Place the salmon in a pan over medium heat. With a spoon or fork, break the salmon chunk in pieces, ensuring not to crush.

Chop the tomato, scallion, shado beni, garlic and onion. Add all the ingredients to the pan with the salmon, bring to a boil then simmer for about 5 minutes.

Tradition: My mom would heat a tablespoon of vegetable oil in a pan, and add the onion, garlic, thyme, cilantro, scallion and black pepper. When it all softened up, she would add the salmon, give it a stir and add all the other ingredients. This would cook for 4-6 minutes. I don't like using the extra oil as I find that salmon is a fatty fish, so I pretty much reversed her method.

Bake and Shark is a classic Trinidad and Tobago street food sandwich. If you've ever had the pleasure of spending a day on the beach at Maracas Bay, I'm sure you may have patronized Richard's or one of the other vendors who make this sandwich so popular.

directions in the "Lime, Lemon or Vinegar!" section of the book. Place in a bowl and season with the salt, black pepper, crushed garlic, green seasoning and finely-chopped scotch bonnet pepper. Give it a good stir and allow to marinate in the fridge for about 30 minutes.

Meanwhile, create a frying station by setting up a plate with flour, a deep pan with vegetable oil and a wire basket (or bowl) lined with paper towels to drain excess oil from finished product.

Heat oil on medium-high. Take each piece of seasoned shark and dust both sides with flour then place gently into the hot oil. Cook in batches, to avoid overcrowding the pan, about 2-3 minutes on each side. Remembering to flip. If you overcook the shark, it may become tough. Remove from oil and drain.

With the Bake you made using the recipe on page 143, assemble your Bake and Shark sandwiches. If you've ever purchased this in Trinidad and Tobago, you'll know the condiments are just as important as the sandwich, so be a bit creative. Top with fresh tomato, red onions, slices of pineapple, fresh lettuce and a variety of sauces.

You'll Need...

- 2 lbs shark
- 1 lime or lemon (to clean shark)
- 1/2 teaspoon salt
- 1/4 teaspoon black pepper
- 2 cloves garlic
- 1 tablespoon green seasoning

- 1/4 scotch bonnet pepper, finely chopped
- 1 cup all-purpose flour
- 2-3 cups vegetable oil

Remove the skin from the shark, remove the meat off the centre bone and slice thinly. Clean shark according to the

Technique: Learn to skin and fillet shark by visiting youtube.com/foodfaq.

Air It Out: I like frying fish outdoors, as the smell can be very strong. If you have a propane grill, using the burner to fry the shark is a great idea.

The biggest thrill for me is visiting local farmers markets when I travel. It really reminds me of those times mom and I would head to 'market day' in the city. Even today, when I go back to the islands, my dad reserves a day for mom and I to check out the market in San Fernando–Trinidad's second largest city."

Here's a vegetarian dish that can be personalized according to your palate, since you can use any vegetables. And if tofu is your thing, hey, add that too. The kebobs are grilled and look attractive, so be prepared to have your guests rush the platter when you serve them. Full of true Caribbean flavour, even the pickiest eaters will be asking for this dish time and time again.

You'll Need...

- Bamboo skewers, soaked in water for 30 minutes prior to grilling to avoid burning
- 1 scotch bonnet pepper
- 2 cloves garlic
- 1 tablespoon shado beni
- 1 sprig thyme
- 2 tablespoons parsley
- 1/3 cup extra virgin olive oil
- 1/2 lemon
- 1/2 teaspoon salt
- 1/2 teaspoon black pepper
- 1 sweet corn on the cob
- 4 different coloured bell peppers
- 1 large red onion
- 8 mushrooms

De-seed the scotch bonnet pepper and give it a fine chop. Chop the garlic, shado beni, thyme and parsley as well. Pour the olive oil into a bowl, squeeze in the lemon juice, and add the salt and black pepper. Whisking the liquid, add the chopped garlic, thyme, shado beni and parsley. If you wish to add additional flavour, do so by splashing in some balsamic vinegar.

Now it's time to prep the vegetables to be marinated. Try to keep all the vegetable pieces the same size so they cook evenly. Peel your corn, remove the silk, give it a wash and cut into 1/2-inch pieces. Wash and remove the seeds from the bell peppers and cut into 1-inch pieces. Peel and dice the red onion. You should keep the onion pieces 2 layers thick so they're as thick as the bell pepper pieces. Wash the mushrooms.

Put everything into a large bowl, pour in the marinade and give it a good mix. Allow to marinate for a couple hours.

Thread your vegetables onto the bamboo skewers, alternating. Get your grill nice and hot (about 375-400 F). Then, holding a vegetable oil-soaked paper towel with tongs, brush the grates or spray with non-stick spray. Place the vegetable skewers onto the grill. Cook for a couple minutes on each side, using the remaining marinade to brush onto the kebabs as they grill. The veggies should have beautiful grill marks and still have a slight crunch when cooked. Remember, they will continue to cook after coming off the grill so do not overcook. The grilling will intensify the natural sugars in the vegetables and with that wicked Caribbean marinade you made, yup, pure niceness!

Wrap It Up: If you're worried about your bamboo skewers burning, you can wrap the exposed ends with tin foil.

A Delectable Corn Soup

Corn Soup is one of those hearty on-the-go meals that you get after fetes (parties/nightclubs), and it has made its way into the fabric of good street food on the islands. Normally, I like my soups with meat in them and there are times when I use salted pigtails in this dish. But this time, we'll go strictly vegetarian. It makes for a very filling and tasty soup your entire family will love—especially if you're based in colder climates and looking for something to warm you on those cold winter nights.

Start by peeling, cutting, chopping and cubing the vegetables and herbs. Cut the corn into 1-inch pieces.

In a large pot, heat the oil on medium heat. Add the diced onions, garlic, celery, herbs and hot pepper. Sauté for a couple minutes then add the split peas and stir well. Add all remaining ingredients, except the pieces of corn and dumplings. Bring that to a boil then reduce to a gentle simmer for 50 minutes, leaving the pot slightly ajar. The idea is to soften the split peas and allow everything else to cook down into a lovely thick soup. Remember to keep stirring.

In the meantime, make the flour dumplings by combining the dumpling ingredients and working into a dough. Add water slowly because you're trying to achieve a firm dough. Allow that to sit for about 10 minutes then pinch off small pieces of dough and, using both hands, roll them into small cigars.

Add the pieces of corn and dumplings to the soup. Allow it to come back up to a boil and let it cook for about 15 minutes. If you notice that the soup is overly thick, feel free to add more water or vegetable stock.

You'll Need...

- 1 large sweet potato
- 4 medium potatoes
- 1 lb pumpkin
- 2-3 corn on the cob
- 1 large onion
- 3 cloves garlic
- 1 large carrot
- 1 cup celery
- 2 tablespoons vegetable oil
- 1 scotch bonnet pepper (or any hot pepper you like)
- 2 tablespoons shado beni
- 2 tablespoons chives
- 3 sprigs thyme

- 2 tablespoons parsley
- 1 cup yellow split peas
- 3 cups vegetable stock
- 3 cups water
- 1/4 teaspoon black pepper
- 3/4 tablespoon salt
- 1 can coconut milk
- 1 can creamed corn

Dumplings...

- 3/4 cup all-purpose flour
- Pinch salt
- Pinch sugar
- About 1/4 cup water (less or more as necessary)

Make It Meaty: If you're making the soup with salted pigtails, remember to pre-boil the pigtails to remove some of the salt. You may not need to add any additional salt, as the salt that remains from the pigtails will be enough to flavour the entire dish.

Ital is the name given to foods enjoyed by the Rastafari community that don't contain any salt or meat. However, consumption of fish, particularly those less than twelve inches in length, is practiced within some Rastafari Ital diets and sea salt can be used in some cases.

To comply with those dietary restrictions, I don't use any form of salt in this recipe. It was a bit challenging to have a well-balanced soup, since my palate is so dependent on the sinful addiction that is salt. But with all the natural seasoning from the fresh herbs, you'll be quite surprised at how tasty this Ital soup is.

You'll Need...

- 1 cup split peas
- 8-10 cups water
- 2 scallions
- 3 cloves garlic
- 1 onion
- 1/2 cup celery
- 1 scotch bonnet pepper
- 1 half-ripe plantain
- 3 eddoes
- 2 potatoes
- 1 medium sweet potato
- 1 carrot
- 1 cup pumpkin
- 2 cups coconut milk
- 6 sprigs thyme
- 1/2 teaspoon black pepper
- 1 tablespoon ginger, freshly grated

(optional)
- 2 tablespoons fresh oregano
- 5 okra
- 2-3 cups callaloo bush

Wash the split peas then place them in a large soup pot and cover with 8 cups of water. As the peas come to a boil, chop the scallion, garlic, onion and celery. Add these flavourful ingredients, reduce to a simmer and let cook for 45 minutes. Also, place the whole scotch bonnet pepper in the pot. You can remove it at the end of the cooking process or, if you like the heat, burst it open to release the Caribbean Sunshine.

As the peas and other ingredients are simmering, peel, cube and wash the plantain, eddoes, potato, sweet potato, carrot and pumpkin. Add them to the pot

at the 45-minute mark. Follow by pouring in the coconut milk, and adding the thyme, black pepper, ginger and oregano. Make sure you have enough liquid in the pot to cover everything. You can add more water or coconut milk, if required. Bring to a boil and reduce to a gentle simmer.

While the soup is simmering, trim the stems off the okra, cut into 1-inch pieces and add to the pot.

20 minutes after adding the okra, everything should almost be cooked all the way through. Wash and trim the callaloo bush, and add it to the pot. Allow to cook for a further 7 minutes so the callaloo can release its flavour and the soup can thicken up. If you're adding salt, now would be a good time to do so (adjust accordingly).

Remove or burst the scotch bonnet pepper and if you added thyme with its sprigs, fish them out as well. Once you ladle the soup into bowls, a nice finishing touch is topping with some freshly squeezed lime juice.

Substitute: If you can't source callaloo bush, feel free to use typical North American spinach, baby dasheen bush leaves or shredded cabbage.

Let It Do Its Thing: This soup will thicken up quite a bit as it cools, so make sure you leave a fair amount of broth to compensate.

This soup follows the North American method of roasting root vegetables to intensify their flavours and to bring out natural sweetness. Since I've been calling Canada home in excess of 20 years, it's only natural that I use this technique. Of course I give the dish a Caribbean twist by adding some richness with coconut milk and ensuring the Caribbean Sunshine (scotch bonnet peppers) makes an appearance. But unlike the heavy soups laden with ground provisions that we are accustomed to in the Caribbean, this one is much lighter yet very filling and quite comforting.

surrounding the seeds, as that's where the raw heat resides.

Allow the roasted vegetables to cool a bit, so you can easily handle them. Once cooled, use a spoon to scoop out all the flesh and place into a soup pot. Remove the skins from the garlic and shallots, and place them in the pot as well.

Add remaining ingredients, bring to a boil and reduce to a simmer for 20 minutes, stirring every 4-5 minutes.

Once the soup cools enough to be safe for pureeing, add it to a blender or use an immersion blender and puree to a smooth and silky consistency. After you adjust for salt, place the soup back in the pot and reheat.

Top with chopped chives and make sure you have some Coconut Bake (see recipe on page146) to enjoy with this lovely roasted vegetarian soup.

You'll Need...

- 1 large sweet potato
- 1 acorn squash (or butternut squash)
- 1 large shallot
- 2 tablespoons olive oil
- 4 cloves garlic (with skin)
- 1/4 scotch bonnet pepper
- 3 cups vegetable stock
- 1/2 teaspoon salt
- Freshly ground black pepper
- 3/4 cup coconut milk

Preheat your oven to 375 F.

Cut the sweet potato, squash and shallot in half. Using a spoon, scoop out and discard the seeds and membrane of the squash. Brush each half of each veggie with olive oil and place, cut side down, on a roasting tray, along with the whole garlic cloves. Place the tray in the oven for about 35-40 minutes.

In the meantime, dice the scotch bonnet pepper very finely. Don't use any of the seeds or white membrane directly

A Dash Of Something Extra: You can add your favourite herbs and top with freshly grated nutmeg and chopped chives.

Serve It Up: There will be enough here for about six people as a side dish or starter, and four people as a complete meal with toasted bread.

This is one of those dishes that my mom couldn't get me and my siblings to eat when we were kids, even if she begged. Aside from when it was in Chow Mein, there were two ways we could be convinced to eat cabbage and they both included adding meat of some sort. First, there was Corned Beef with Cabbage (see recipe on page 63). Second, there was leftover Stew Pork with Cabbage.

Our dad also tried, in vain, to convince us to eat cabbage when my mom would add saltfish to it but...nah!

Start by shredding the cabbage as you would for coleslaw, but a little thicker. Give it a quick rinse under cool water and shake off as much of the water as you are able to.

In a pan, heat the oil on medium then add half of the sliced onion, garlic and hot pepper. Allow that to cook for a couple of minutes then lower the heat, add the curry powder and stir. Cook for another 2-3 minutes before you add the water. The idea now is to cook the curry powder to release its aroma then make a quick paste by cooking off all the water, until it goes dark and grainy.

Add the shredded cabbage, remaining onion and salt. Give it a good stir and turn the heat to low. Cook for about 20-25 minutes, with the pot uncovered or risk having the cabbage spring a lot of liquid and get soupy. I like the cabbage to have a slight crunch to it. However, if you wish, you can cook it a little longer. If you'd like a bit of contrast, during the last 5 minutes add tomato slices. Remember to taste for salt.

You'll Need...

- 1/4 large cabbage (about 4 cups), shredded
- 1 tablespoon olive oil (or vegetable oil)
- 1 medium onion, sliced and divided
- 2 cloves garlic, thinly sliced
- 1/4 scotch bonnet pepper (or habanero)
- 1/4 cup water
- 1 teaspoon curry powder
- 1/2 teaspoon salt
- 1 sliced tomato (optional, but adds contrast and colour)

Mom's method: In the second step, my mom combines water and curry powder in a bowl to make a paste before adding it to the pan. For her method, see the "Variety of the Spice of Life—And Curry" section of the book.

Stewed Caribbean-Style Lentils

Lentils are one of the best vegetable sources of iron. This makes them an important part of a vegetarian diet and useful for preventing iron deficiency. I usually make lentils in a huge batch so I can enjoy some right away and freeze the rest for later. Freezing them is also a great idea because lentils take a while to cook if you don't have a pressure cooker. I've had Stewed Caribbean-Style Lentils last up to three months in the freezer and once reheated, they tasted the same as the day they were cooked.

You'll Need...

- 2 cups small brown lentils
- Water (see directions)
- 3 cloves garlic
- Scotch bonnet pepper (to your liking)
- 3/4 teaspoon salt
- 2 sprigs thyme
- Dash black pepper
- 1 tablespoon vegetable oil
- 1 onion, sliced
- 1/2 teaspoon Caribbean-style browning
- 1 scallion, thinly sliced
- 2 tablespoons shado beni, chopped
- 1/2 tablespoon Caribbean salted butter

Optional Ingredients...
- 2 carrots, diced
- 1 bell pepper, diced
- 1 tomato, diced

Go through the lentils to ensure there's no debris (I've seen little pebbles and twigs). Pour the lentils into a bowl, wash with cool water and drain. Add enough water to the bowl to cover the lentils and allow to soak for a couple hours or overnight, which would be best.

Pour the lentils and water into a deep pot. Add additional water so everything is covered by at least 2 inches. With the heat on medium, add the garlic, scotch bonnet pepper, salt, thyme and black pepper. If you're using the optional ingredients, add them now. Bring this to a boil then cover and reduce heat to a low simmer. Allow to cook for about 45 minutes or until the lentils are tender. After the lentils are tender, pay attention to the amount of water in your pot because you don't want the mixture to get too thick or all the water to burn off. If you find that it's starting to get overly thick, add a cup of water.

In another saucepan on medium, heat oil. Add sliced onions and cook for a couple of minutes, until the onions are soft and start getting golden edges. Then gently, as you're mixing liquid with hot oil, add the cooked lentils to the saucepan.

With a whisk or swizzle stick, whisk or swizzle everything to break down the lentils a bit. Add the browning, scallions, shado beni and Caribbean salted butter, and stir. Allow this to cook for a couple minutes more.

Don't forget to fish out the sprig of thyme before serving. You're aiming for a thick, soup-like consistency.

Authenticity: Caribbean salted butter (a.k.a. the Golden Ray brand) is uniquely different from traditional butter. It has a wonderful Creole flavour, which adds a distinct twist to the finished product. This butter can be found at West Indian and some Asian supermarkets.

The Ultimate Breadfruit Pie

I grew up eating breadfruit in a number of ways. But it was only when I visited Tobago some years ago that I had my first encounter with delicious Breadfruit Pie. After a long day of driving around the island, my family and I stopped at Jemma's Seaview Kitchen for a late lunch and Breadfruit Pie with stewed fish really hit the spot. With the soothing sound of waves crashing just feet away, the sleepies kicked in.

You'll Need...

- 1 breadfruit (about 4 lbs)
- 1/4 teaspoon salt
- 3 tablespoons butter
- 3 tablespoons all-purpose flour
- 1 1/2 cups evaporated milk
- 2 tablespoons parsley, chopped
- 1 cup medium cheddar cheese, grated
- 1/2 cup Monterey Jack cheese, grated
- 1/2 cup onion, finely diced
- 1 tablespoon powdered mustard
- 1/4 scotch bonnet pepper, finely diced
- Pinch nutmeg
- 1/4 teaspoon black pepper

Cut the stem off the breadfruit. Rest, flat side down, on your counter and cut into wedges. Peel off the skin with a potato peeler or paring knife. Lastly, remove the sort of spongy centre (almost like the continuation of the stem), so you're left with wedges.

Place the breadfruit wedges in a deep pot and cover with water. Bring to a boil, salt and allow to cook until they're tender, about 20 minutes. You'll know the breadfruit is fully cooked if you pierce with a sharp knife and there's no resistance. Drain and set aside to cool a bit.

In another saucepan, on low, heat the butter. As it melts, add the flour and cook for about 4-5 minutes. It's important that you constantly whisk it, so the flour does not clump or burn. Add the evaporated milk, turn the heat up to medium and whisk. Add all the other ingredients (except the breadfruit and about 1/4 cup cheddar

cheese) and cook for a couple minutes until you have a thick but smooth sauce. If it's overly thick, add about 1/4 cup more milk, cream or water.

Cut each wedge of cooked breadfruit into slices about 1/4-inch thick and place a layer in a greased baking dish. Add a layer of cheese sauce then another layer of sliced breadfruit and top with the remaining cheese sauce. Sprinkle with the reserved cheddar cheese.

Place the baking dish on the middle rack of a pre-heated 350 F oven and bake for about 30 minutes. If the Pie is not golden after this time, place it under the broiler for 2-3 minutes. Allow the Breadfruit Pie to cool for 10 minutes before serving.

Personalize: You can use your favourite type of cheese to personalize this dish. It can also be topped with bread crumbs.

Aloo Choka

In true Caribbean style, we have our own version of the classic North American side dish Garlic Mashed Potatoes. I fell in love with Garlic Mash when I first moved to Canada. It's one of those sides I get whenever I go out for steak dinner—maybe because it reminds me of the Aloo Choka I enjoyed as a boy. If you're new to Caribbean cooking or you're not familiar with places in the West Indies influenced by India, aloo is just another word for potato.

Peel, wash and cut the potatoes in halves. Place in a deep pot and cover with unsalted water. Bring to a boil and cook until tender (when a fork can go through without any resistance), about 15-20 minutes.

Meanwhile, in a bowl, place salt, garlic and hot pepper, and crush to a smooth paste. You can also use a mortar and pestle.

After the potatoes are cooked, drain and add to the bowl with the garlic paste. Mash until it's smooth and free of any lumps.

Top potatoes with thinly sliced onion, but don't mix or stir yet. Heat the oil on medium-high until it's hot (just about to smoke). Drizzle directly over the onion slices and the top of the mashed potatoes. This will semi-cook the onion and release some of its distinct flavours into the bowl. Give everything a good stir, check for salt and serve.

More Garlic: I've seen people add a clove of thinly sliced garlic into the frying pan with the hot oil to cook for a minute before adding to the bowl with the mashed potatoes.

Kick It Up: I like using a "green" hot pepper, as the flavour is a bit different than a fully ripe pepper. Plus, the green specks in the finished dish give it some character.

You'll Need...

- 4 large potatoes
- 1/2 teaspoon salt
- 1 clove garlic
- 1/4 green scotch bonnet (see Kick It Up note)
- 1/4 onion, thinly sliced
- 3 tablespoons olive oil
- 1 clove garlic, sliced (optional)

Cheesy Cassava Mash

Like my dad and my younger brother, I'm a huge fan of ground provisions. So, I'm always trying to come up with different ways to enjoy their earthy goodness. In this recipe, instead of using the typical potato, I experimented with cassava and came up with a delicious Cheesy Cassava Mash. It's enhanced with the wonderful nuttiness of aged cheddar.

and remove the woody vein. Rinse the cassava and cut into similarly sized pieces.

In a deep pot, cover cassava with cool water, bring to a boil, add salt then reduce to a rolling boil. If any foam accumulates on the surface of the water, spoon off and discard. Allow the cassava to cook until it's tender, which may take 20-25 minutes. Every cassava cooks differently for some reason, so a good test is to pierce with a sharp knife. If there's no resistance, it means the cassava is fully cooked and you can drain.

Add all remaining ingredients to the pot with the cassava and mash to the consistency you like. Remember to taste for salt and you can certainly play around with the amount and type of cheese you use. Some grated Parmesan would be a nice touch.

Time-Saver: If you want to skip having to peel the cassava, check the frozen section of most grocery stores for peeled cassava. If you are using frozen cassava, follow the cooking instructions on the package.

Labour Of Love: This is a heavy mash—not light as with potatoes. So, be cautious if you plan on using a hand mixer to whip it.

Safety First: When working with raw ground provisions, be sure to either wear gloves or rub some vegetable oil on your hands. You may find that your hands will itch if you don't.

You'll Need...

- 2 1/2-3 lbs cassava
- 1/2 teaspoon salt
- 1/2 cup evaporated milk (room temperature)
- 1/2 cup aged cheddar cheese, grated
- 1/4 teaspoon black pepper
- 1 tablespoon butter
- Pinch nutmeg

Remove the top and bottom of the cassava, and discard. Cut the provision into 3-inch pieces, lengthwise. Using a paring knife or potato peeler, remove the outer skin. It will be a bit tough. What I normally do is cut a slit into the skin then place the blade of my paring knife to sort of lift the skin away from the flesh of the cassava. Once they're peeled, cut the cassava pieces lengthwise down the centre

Classic Island Rice and Peas

This Rice and Peas dish is normally associated with Jamaica—and quite rightly so. However, just about every island in the Caribbean has its own version. My daughters refer to this dish as "the spicy rice with the beanies". Peas or beans have always been called "beanies" and they use the word "spicy" because I love to burst the scotch bonnet pepper near the end of cooking to release all that wonderful Caribbean vibe!

You'll Need...

- 1/2 cup dried red kidney beans
- 2 cups water
- 2 scallions
- 1 onion
- 2 cloves garlic
- 1/2 teaspoon salt
- 1/4 teaspoon black pepper
- 1/4 teaspoon ground allspice
- 3 sprigs thyme
- 1 scotch bonnet pepper
- 2 cups long grain brown rice
- 1 1/2 cups coconut milk

Go through the dried kidney beans to remove any debris (I've seen little pebbles and twigs). Rinse well with cool water, drain and place in a bowl. Add 2 cups of water and allow to soak for a couple of hours or even overnight.

Pour the beans and water in which they've been soaking into a deep saucepan and bring to a boil. Chop the scallions, onion and garlic, and add to the pot as well. Then, drop in the salt, black pepper, allspice and the sprigs of thyme. Don't worry about the sprigs, as you can remove them when the dish is done. Before lowering your heat to a simmer, drop the whole scotch bonnet pepper into the pot. This will give you a ton of flavour. Place the lid on your pot and reduce to a gentle simmer. Depending on how long you pre-soaked your beans, it will take about 40 minutes-1 hour for them to become tender so you can add the rice.

While your beans are plumping up and the

water is taking on a lovely reddish hue (this will help create that unique Rice and Peas colour), prepare your rice. To do so, wash it according to the directions in the "Wash That Rice Right" section of the book.

Add the washed rice to the pot with the plump beans and give it a good stir before adding the coconut milk and bringing back to a boil. Once boiling, reduce the heat to a gentle simmer, put the lid on the pot and allow to cook. Depending on the rice you used (no two brands cook the same), it can take 25-35 minutes to fully cook. The liquid will slowly burn off as the rice

cooks, so keep an eye on things. I like my Rice and Peas grainy but if you like the rice a bit creamier, you may need a bit more liquid and cooking time. In the event your rice is not fully cooked after 25-35 minutes, simply add a bit more water or coconut milk and continue to cook.

Once the rice is cooked, remove the sprigs of thyme and don't forget that scotch bonnet pepper. You can certainly burst it open and release the heat or fish it out and discard. However, I'm sure one of your family members or friends may appreciate the pepper, so set it aside for them.

Rich And Creamy Pumpkin Rice

Pumpkin rice is a dish I only started to appreciate after having it at an Island Grill fast food joint in Kingston, Jamaica. When I was growing up, my dad would praise this dish and how well it went with pieces of saltfish. I have to agree.

You'll Need...

- 2 cups pumpkin
- 2 cloves garlic
- 1 medium onion
- 1/2 teaspoon ginger
- 1 tablespoon olive oil (or vegetable oil or butter)
- 2-3 sprigs thyme
- 1/4 teaspoon black pepper
- 2 cups long grain brown rice
- 3 - 3 1/2 cups vegetable stock
- 1 teaspoon salt (or more, to taste)
- 1 whole scotch bonnet pepper

Peel and dice the pumpkin, garlic and onion, and grate the ginger. Set aside.

In a deep pot, heat the oil on medium-high, and add the diced onion, garlic and the thyme. Allow this to soften up for a couple of minutes. Add the grated ginger and black pepper to the pot, and give it a good stir. Add the pumpkin pieces and give it another good stir. Turn your heat to medium-low and allow this to cook for a couple of minutes to release all the wonderful flavours.

Meanwhile, wash your rice according to directions in the "Wash That Rice Right"

section of the book.

With the rice washed and drained, add it to the pot and stir. Pour in the stock, add salt and pop in the scotch bonnet pepper. Bring to a boil then reduce to a simmer and cover the pot with its lid to cook off the liquid, and get the rice nice and tender.

After about 10 minutes, you'll notice that your liquid has been reduced, the pieces of pumpkin are starting to fall apart and the rice grains are becoming plump. If after 18 minutes, you notice that the rice grains are almost completely cooked but you still have some liquid, turn up the heat and burn off the liquid. Remember to stir or the rice will stick to the bottom of the pot. I like my rice a bit grainy so I have to account for it cooking in its own heat, even after I turn off the stove. If you like your rice creamy, allow more cooking time to really plump it up. The texture and consistency of the final product will depend on your liking. Check for salt and if you'd like, add more. Remember to remove the scotch bonnet pepper at the end. If, however, you want a blast of heat, burst open the pepper—but be prepared for its wickedness.

Kick It Up: By using the whole scotch bonnet pepper in the dish, I got the flavour but not the heat.

Substitute: I use calabaza (Cucurbita moschata), also known as West Indian, Cuban or Caribbean pumpkin. Butternut squash would make an excellent substitute.

Vegetable Fried Rice

My mom makes deadly fried rice with chicken or shrimp, but my sister is still the best when it comes to tasty Shrimp Fried Rice. It is something we look forward to during family gatherings. In this recipe, I avoided meat. But with the layers of flavours, you'll be amazed at how scrumptious the Vegetable Fried Rice turns out.

minutes. Add diced carrots (as this is the only vegetable that will take longer to cook), stir and cook for a couple minutes. Add diced onion, bell pepper and celery. Allow to cook for a couple minutes.

Add the black pepper, soy sauce and sesame oil. Everything will go dark, but have no fear. Once you add the cooked rice, the colour will balance off. Add the frozen peas and give it a stir.

Gradually add the cooked but chilled rice, stirring to make sure all rice grains get evenly coated with the dark base. If you find that the colour is not dark enough for you, just add more soy sauce. Soy sauce is salty, so if you do add more, adjust accordingly the amount of salt, which you can add now. All you're doing is basically heating through the rice, so within 4-5 minutes, it should be done. Turn off the stove, add chopped scallions and give everything a good final stir.

You'll Need...

- **2 tablespoons vegetable oil**
- **3 cloves garlic, crushed**
- **1/2 teaspoon ginger, grated**
- **1 cup carrot, diced**
- **1 large onion, diced**
- **1/2 cup bell pepper, diced**
- **1/2 cup celery, diced**
- **3 tablespoons dark soy sauce**
- **1/4 teaspoon black pepper**
- **1/2 teaspoon sesame oil**
- **1 cup frozen peas**
- **4 cups rice, cooked and chilled**
- **3/4 teaspoon salt**
- **2 scallions, chopped**

In a wide pan or wok, heat vegetable oil on medium-high. Add crushed garlic and grated ginger. Give it a good stir, as you're trying to release all the wonderful flavours to create a base. Cook for 1-2

Rice Prep: I use long-grain brown rice, which I cook without salt and remove from the stove about five minutes before it is fully cooked. Additionally, I allow it to cool, overnight, in the fridge. These two elements are the tricks to having grainy Vegetable Fried Rice that will not clump or go soggy.

Size Matters Try to keep the vegetable pieces uniform in size to allow for even cooking. Nothing should be too big, as everything needs to cook fast.

Everyday Cornmeal Dumplings

This is one of those meals I refer to as "country food" because of its rustic feel and simplicity. As a kid, one of my favourite "bush cook" meals was these dumplings with a side of Dasheen Bush Bhaji, cooked in coconut milk. It was a meal that was guaranteed to give you the sleepies after you ate a huge plate. The dumplings in the photo you see here are topped with Smoked Herring Buljol. You can find that recipe on CaribbeanPot.com.

You'll Need...

- **1 cup all-purpose flour**
- **1/2 cup cornmeal**
- **1 teaspoon granulated sugar**
- **1 1/2 teaspoons baking powder**
- **Pinch cinnamon**
- **Lukewarm water**

This is so simple you'll be done in less than 20 minutes. Add all the ingredients except the water to a bowl and give it a good whisk to mix everything. Then start adding a bit of the lukewarm water at a time and mix until you have dough that is firm yet soft. Knead for about 2-3 minutes.

Pinch off a piece (the size will depend on how large you want your finished dumplings, since they swell as they boil) and shape into a small cigar. Once you've rolled all the dough into cigars, flatten each one out from the centre until you have dumplings that are almost oval in shape.

Place the dumplings into a pot of about 8 cups of boiling water with 1/2 teaspoon salt and cook for about 15 minutes. They will get bigger in size and float when they're fully cooked. Drain and serve while still warm.

Serve 'Em Up: If you don't have a topping for these Everyday Cornmeal Dumplings, you can certainly toss them in some butter or olive oil and crack in some fresh black pepper. You can also top them with Saltfish Buljol, Caribbean-style stewed meats or any of the vegetarian type sides in this book. Lastly, they are excellent in those heavy soups we enjoy on the islands.

Jamaican Festival: The Fundamental Fried Dumpling

My first encounter with truly good Festival was several years ago during breakfast at my friend Dino's home in Portmore, Jamaica—at the same time I fell in love with Ackee and Saltfish (see recipe on page 82). Imagine waking up to a full spread of Festival, Ackee and Saltfish, boiled green bananas and to top it all off, a piping hot cup of rich and creamy Milo! Moms (Dino's mom) had us set for the day. When the time came for us to continue our trek through Jamaica (to Ocho Rios, Montego Bay and Negril), it was painful to know that we wouldn't be waking up to such a wonderful home-cooked breakfast anymore.

Jamaican Festival is just amazing and you'll love the crunchy exterior and the fluffy interior followed by the flavoured sweetness of vanilla and sugar.

You'll Need...

- 1 1/2 cups all-purpose flour
- 1 teaspoon baking powder
- 3 tablespoons cornmeal
- 3 tablespoons white sugar
- 1/2 teaspoon salt
- 1/2 cup water
- 1 teaspoon vanilla
- About 3 cups vegetable oil

In a large bowl, sift the flour and baking powder then add the cornmeal, sugar and salt. Give that a quick whisk to combine.

Mix the water and vanilla together then start adding a little at a time, as you whisk, to the bowl with the dry ingredients. When it starts to take the shape of dough, you will need to get your hands in there and start kneading. If you find that the 1/2 cup of water is not enough, drizzle in some more. The idea is to work it for 5-7 minutes, until you have a well-formed dough ball that's firm and slightly sticky. Cover with plastic wrap or a tea towel and allow the dough to rest for about 30 minutes.

Dust your work surface with flour and, as best as you can, divide the dough ball into 8 equal parts. Using your hands, form each piece into a cigar shape. Try to make them about 6-8 inches long and not overly thick because the Festival will increase in size when fried.

Heat the vegetable oil on medium then gently add the shaped dough into the pan. Allow to fry for about 2-3 minutes before you flip over the Festival. In total, you'll need between 5-6 minutes for each to be fully cooked and take on a lovely golden colour. Have paper towels ready to drain off the excess oil after they're fried.

Try to serve warm. And if you want to get a bit creative, dust the Festival with some icing sugar to make it a sweet snack. The kids will love it.

Trinbago Aloo Pie

As I mentioned before, "aloo" simply means potato and though this is called a pie, it's not what most people outside of Trinidad and Tobago envision when they hear the word. Aloo Pie is basically a deep-fried dough pocket filled with potato. It's one of the many quick delights you can buy from street food vendors throughout the islands.

You'll Need...

Filling...
- 4 medium potatoes
- 1/4 teaspoon salt
- 1 clove garlic
- 1/4 hot pepper (optional)
- 1/4 teaspoon roasted cumin powder

Dough...
- 1 3/4 cups all-purpose flour
- Pinch salt
- Pinch self-rising yeast
- 1/3-3/4 cup water
- About 2 cups vegetable oil

Peel and cut the potatoes in half. In a pot with enough water to cover, bring to boil and then turn heat to medium-low to allow potatoes to cook gently, about 15 minutes or until you can pierce with a knife without any real resistance.

In the meantime, place all the dough ingredients in a bowl and add 1/2 of the water. Work well and add more water as needed. You're looking for a dough that's smooth and somewhat firm. Allow this to rest, in a bowl covered with plastic wrap, at least 15 minutes at room temperature.

The potatoes should be fully cooked now. In a bowl, add the salt, garlic and hot pepper and crush to a fine paste (you can also use a mortar and pestle for this). Once crushed, add to the cooked potatoes and mash. The goal is to have a smooth texture without any lumps. Lastly, add the cumin and stir well to combine.

Pull the rested dough apart into 4 or 5 small balls. Dust your work surface with flour and using a rolling pin, roll out to form small circles—about 6-8 inches in diameter. Place some of the potato filling on half of a dough circle, but leave room around the edges because you will be sealing it. Flip the unfilled side over and using a fork, press down to make a seal. You're essentially making a half-circle, dough-filled package. When you've sealed with the fork, flip over and do the same thing on the other side, as you want to be sure it doesn't open during the frying process. Repeat until all dough circles are filled and sealed.

In a pan, heat the oil on medium-high and carefully add two pies at a time.

Within seconds, flip onto the other side. This quick action helps to achieve a perfectly shaped pie. Cook for 2-3 minutes before flipping back to the side on which you started for another 2-3 minutes. You're looking to get a golden-brown colour. If you find the pies going dark fast, turn down the heat. Repeat until all pies are fried. Drain on paper towels and serve warm.

Perfect Partner: Traditionally, Aloo Pie is served with spicy chutney. Try it with my Spicy Cucumber Chutney, which you can find on page 122.

Typical Trinbagonian Pholourie

These tasty snack bites can be addictive, especially if you have them right after they're done. When I was in primary school, I always used my daily allowance to get a few during recess. The many vendors outside of the school's compound offered a variety of snack foods. It would be safe to say that I grew up on Pholourie.

about 30 minutes.

In a fairly deep frying pan, add enough oil to deep fry. Heat on medium-high. While the oil heats, get a basket or bowl and line with paper towels to absorb the excess oil from the Pholourie. Also, get your long-handle tongs to avoid being burned by oil splatter.

When the oil is hot, scoop a tablespoonful of batter and place into the hot oil. Use a second spoon to scrape the batter off the original spoon. After a few seconds, using tongs, flip over. You're looking for a golden-brown colour and the Pholourie will start floating when the centre is fully cooked, about 5 minutes. You'll notice that each Pholourie will easily double in size as it cooks, so don't crowd the pan.

Don't worry if the first batch turns out a bit deformed in shape, you'll quickly get the hang of it. Remove from the oil and place on the paper towels, repeat until all batter is used.

You'll Need...

- 2 cloves garlic
- 1 teaspoon salt
- 1/4 scotch bonnet or any hot pepper, crushed (optional)
- 1 cup all-purpose flour
- 1 teaspoon baking powder
- 1 cup ground split pea powder
- 1 teaspoon turmeric
- 1 1/3 cups water
- 2 cups vegetable oil

Place 2 cloves of garlic, salt and hot pepper into a mortar. The coarse texture of the salt works great to help crush the pepper and garlic. Using the pestle, create a smooth paste. Set aside.

In a large bowl, place the flour, baking powder, split pea powder and turmeric, and whisk. After the dry ingredients are incorporated, add the crushed garlic paste and water. Mix thoroughly to form a lump-free batter and allow to sit for

Perfect Partner: These are best served with spicy chutney.

☞ **Many chutney recipes can be found at caribbeanpot.com/recipe-index/.**

Servings: This batter makes about 20 to 25 Pholourie, depending on how big you make them.

I grew up in a Catholic home but as is the norm in Trinidad and Tobago, we recognize everyone's religious celebrations equally. So, we would always go down the road to my mom's cousin's house for goodies on Divali (or Diwali, depending on who you ask) night. I looked forward to roti, curry channa with potato, Pholourie and, of course, Saheena. I was never into the sweets but my brother and sisters would do some damage when the sweets tray came around.

You'll Need...

- 1 bunch baby spinach
- 3 cups all-purpose flour
- 1/2 cup split pea powder
- 1 teaspoon salt
- 1/4 teaspoon turmeric
- 1/4 teaspoon roasted cumin powder
- 1/4 teaspoon amchar masala (optional)
- 1 clove garlic, grated
- 1/2 teaspoon baking powder
- 1/4 teaspoon instant yeast
- 1 3/4 cups water
- 2-3 cups vegetable oil

Mango chutney...
- 1 green mango
- 4-6 leaves shado beni
- 1 scotch bonnet pepper
- 2 cloves garlic
- 1/2 cup water
- 1 teaspoon salt

Rinse spinach leaves, roll into little bundles and slice very thinly. Place spinach in a strainer and pour about 3 cups boiling water to blanch or pre-cook.

In a large bowl, place flour, split pea powder, salt, turmeric, cumin, amchar masala, garlic, baking powder and instant yeast. Squeeze liquid from the blanched spinach and add it to the bowl. Add the water and mix into a smooth batter. When everything is fully incorporated, cover the bowl with plastic wrap and allow to rest for 2 hours (the yeast will activate, doubling the dough in size).

Meanwhile, set up a frying station with oil in a deep pan or pot and a paper-towel lined plate for draining excess oil.

Heat the oil on medium-high. Using a tablespoon, scoop a spoonful of batter into the pan and use a second spoon to scrape off leftover batter. Fry for about 4-5 minutes, moving as you do. If you find the dough turning brown fast, lower the heat a bit so the inside cooks evenly.

Place the Saheena on paper towels for draining and make Mango Chutney.

Remove the skin from a green mango (one that's not ripe), slice and discard pit. In a food processor or blender, place mango and all other Mango Chutney ingredients, and puree into an even consistency. Taste for salt and if you find that it's sour or tart, add a dash of sugar to help balance it. In a sealed container in the fridge, this chutney will keep for a few days.

Authenticity: I use baby spinach in this recipe, but traditionally baby dasheen leaves are used.

Cheese Paste
Sandwich Spread

This has got to be one of the simplest recipes I've ever shared and, quite honestly, it's one of my faves! If you're from the Caribbean and you've never had a Cheese Paste sandwich for lunch, your mommy didn't love you. I'm just joking, but just about everyone I speak to about Cheese Paste sandwiches can relate—no matter which island they're from. Cheese Paste is simply a spiced up cheese spread that's ideal on sliced bread or crackers.

Back in the day, people even added a drop or two of food colouring—green, pink, yellow and in some cases, blue—to this wonderful cheesy spread to enhance the look of the finished sandwich. Do you remember?

as you can because you want the overall texture of the Cheese Paste to be very smooth and creamy.

Place all of the ingredients in a large bowl and mix very well. You want to fully incorporate all the flavours and give the cheese paste a lovely "whipped" finish.

Make It Easy: To make the old cheddar cheese easier to grate, firm it up a bit by placing it in the freeze for about 10 minutes before getting started. Also, if you begin to combine the ingredients and the mixture isn't becoming smooth, add 1-2 tablespoons of milk as you whisk.

Substitute And Add: You can certainly use a mixture of different cheeses, if you like. I use what I have in the fridge. You can also further enhance the flavour of the Cheese Paste by adding some finely diced pimento peppers to the mix.

Storage: There will be enough Paste here for about six to eight sandwiches (depending on how thick you spread it on). If you don't use all of the Cheese Paste at once, it can be stored in the fridge for a couple days. Be sure to cover it with plastic wrap or place it in an airtight container.

You'll Need...

- 3 cups old cheddar cheese
- 2 tablespoons carrots, grated
- 1 tablespoon mayo
- 1 tablespoon butter (room temperature)

- Pinch black pepper
- 1/2 small onion, grated
- 1 tablespoon prepared mustard
- Dash hot sauce

Grate the old cheddar cheese as finely

If We Did Guacamole

A few years back, my cousin jokingly said to me, "My wife made me guacamole and roti for breakfast." After the laughter subsided, I realized that he might have a point. What we lovingly call Zaboca Choka in Trinidad and Tobago is pretty close to guacamole. So, here's my take on a Caribbean version of guacamole.

To prevent the avocados from discolouring, add lime juice and give it a good stir.

Add the cubed mango to the bowl and combine.

Add the chopped shado beni and top with finely diced onions but don't stir.

On medium, heat the oil and just before you start seeing smoke, pour it directly onto the diced onions. This will help remove some of the rawness, so the dip doesn't give you karate breath. Stir well and serve or chill in the fridge. Get some corn chips or toast some flatbread and your guests will be praising you, for sure!

Substitute: I use Mexican avocados even though the texture is a bit different than the avocados we have in the Caribbean. Secondly, if you can't source shado beni, use 1/2 cup chopped cilantro. Lastly, if you don't have a red onion, use any sweet onion. Everyday cooking onion, however, may be a bit too strong for this particular recipe.

Servings and Storage: This recipe makes enough to serve about 8-10 people. In the refrigerator, it can last about a day or so. Remember to use the lime juice to prevent discolouration. Lemon works just as well.

Kick It Up: If you love heat, do add a bit more scotch bonnet pepper.

You'll Need...

- 1/4 scotch bonnet pepper
- 1 clove garlic
- 1/4 teaspoon salt
- 4 ripe avocados, peeled and diced
- Juice of 2 limes
- 3/4 cup ripe but firm mango, peeled and diced
- 2 tablespoons shado beni, chopped
- 3/4 cup red onion, diced
- 1 tablespoon olive oil

Using a mortar and pestle, crush the scotch bonnet pepper, garlic and salt into a somewhat smooth paste. Place this wicked spicy paste into a deep bowl, and add the peeled and diced avocados to it. Using the back of a fork, crush the avocados until you have a chunky texture (you can make it as smooth as you like).

Caribbean Spiced Nuts

This book would not be complete if I didn't share one of my dad's favourite snacks. Roasted with a wonderful glaze for a crunchy texture and spiced with some lovely Caribbean elements, this mosaic of nuts is simply outstanding. However, I must warn you that you or anyone who samples these Caribbean Spiced Nuts won't be able to stop at just a handful. So, if you serve them at your next party, be prepared for the bowl to disappear in front of your eyes as your guests zero in. This snack is very similar to beer or honey roasted peanuts but has more flare!

You'll Need...

Glaze...
- 2 tablespoons butter
- 1/2 cup sugar
- 1/4 cup water

- 1 cup unsalted peanuts
- 1 cup raw pecan halves
- 1 cup unsalted almonds, dry roasted
- 1 cup unsalted cashews, dry roasted
- 1 teaspoon salt
- 1/2 teaspoon freshly ground black pepper
- 1/4 teaspoon cumin
- 1/4 teaspoon scotch bonnet pepper, very finely chopped
- 1/4 teaspoon curry powder

Glaze: In a saucepan, place the butter, sugar and water. On medium heat, bring this mix to a boil then lower to a simmer, whisk and cook for 1 minute.

Empty all of the nuts into a large metal bowl and toss in the other dry ingredients, mix well. Pour in the glaze you created and toss everything together. The idea is to coat each nut with the glaze and spices.

Prepare to use your oven's middle rack then preheat the oven to 350 F. Line a cookie sheet with tin foil and spray with cooking spray or brush on some vegetable oil. Pour the now-coated nuts onto the lined sheet and spread evenly in single layer.

Place in the oven for 10 minutes then remove and toss. There will be melted glaze on the lined cookie sheet, which you want pick up as you move the nuts around. It will take a couple of minutes and you will notice that the nuts may start to clump together and form a coating at the same time.

Place back in the oven for an additional 6 minutes. Allow to cool then transfer to a serving bowl and enjoy. Your kitchen will have the lovely scent of freshly roasted nuts, and the spices you used will only enhance this captivating aroma. Store in an airtight container.

Heat Control: The scotch bonnet pepper will give this snack a subtle kick. Don't include any of the seeds from the pepper, as the heat will be very intense. If you're still overly concerned, you can tame things with a touch of paprika and cayenne instead.

Safety First: When chopping the scotch bonnet pepper, wear gloves or coat your hands with a bit of oil.

Fry Channa is one of those spicy snacks sold—in either cone shaped paper packages or reused bottles—by street vendors all over Trinidad. However, my connection to Fry Channa goes back to my mom's cousin's home when, during Divali, she would have a huge bowl for us to snack on while the various vegetarian culinary delights made their way to the table.

The traditional way of making this snack is to fry the channa (chickpeas) in vegetable oil, drain, then season. I've switched it up just a bit. Though this is not the traditional way of making Fry Channa, I find that roasting the chickpeas with the olive oil and seasoning is just spectacular.

Pour the chickpeas into a large bowl and using a paper towel or kitchen towel, dry to get any remaining moisture. Stir the seasoned oil and add it to the bowl with the chickpeas. Sprinkle with the tablespoon of salt and give the entire batch another good stir. The idea is to coat each chickpea with the seasoning.

Preheat your oven to 350 F. Pour the seasoned chickpeas onto a lined baking sheet and arrange in a single layer. Place on the middle rack of the oven and bake for 50 minutes to get a beautiful golden colour and lovely crunch.

These can be enjoyed out of the oven or even days after. However, it's important that you store them in an airtight container to maintain freshness.

Translation: Channa is just another word for chickpeas or garbanzo beans.

Substitute: If you don't have fresh scotch bonnet pepper, you can certainly use pepper sauce or cayenne powder. Also, if you can't source shado beni, use cilantro.

Calling All Salt Lovers: Depending on your fondness of salt, you can dust the chickpeas with additional salt when they first come out of the oven for that unique salted texture that Fry Channa usually has.

You'll Need...

- 2 cups dried chickpeas (channa)
- 4 cups water
- 3 cloves garlic
- 2 tablespoons shado beni
- 1/4 scotch bonnet pepper, de-seeded
- 1 1/2 tablespoons extra virgin olive oil
- 1/4 teaspoon black pepper
- 1 tablespoon salt

Soak the chickpeas overnight in a large bowl of water.

Drain whatever water is left, rinse and place in a colander to fully drain off. You're trying to get the chickpeas as dry as possible before seasoning.

In the meantime, chop the garlic, shado beni and scotch bonnet pepper very finely. Then, into a small bowl, pour the olive oil and add the garlic, shado beni and pepper.

I first sampled Tostones a few years ago when I got off a cruise ship in San Juan, Puerto Rico and stopped at a roadside vendor selling these twice-fried green plantain chips. Served with mojo (garlic sauce), the crispy texture followed by the sort of creamy inside, combined with the plantain's sweet undertones, was just amazing.

If you like potato chips, you'll love these Tostones with their crispy edges. They can be enjoyed on their own, with your favourite dip or as a side to any dish you normally serve.

You'll Need...

- **2 green (unripe) plantains**
- **About 2 cups vegetable oil**
- **Sea salt, to taste**

Trim off both ends of each plantain and discard. Using a paring knife, run a cut length-wise along the natural ridges of each plantain (the thickness of the skin). Then, using a butter knife, place the blade in the cut and peel back the skin. Finally, cut the peeled plantains into 1-inch pieces and set aside in a bowl of cool water so they don't discolour.

In a fairly deep saucepan, heat the oil on medium-high. While it heats, drain the plantain pieces and pat dry with paper towels. Fry them in the hot oil for about 4 minutes, making sure to flip so they cook evenly on both sides. Drain on paper towels and allow them to cool for a couple minutes.

Meanwhile, get a bit of parchment paper and a can (I use a can of soup). Fold the paper in two and place a piece of the fried plantain between the two halves. Using a little force, press down with the can to flatten the plantain. Repeat until all pieces are done.

Return the flattened plantain pieces to the hot oil for about 2 minutes, drain, sprinkle with a bit of sea salt and enjoy.

Tools: There's an actual Tostone press you can purchase for this, but I find a soup can works great. You can even press with your hands if you want, just be sure they've cooled before you do.

Safety First: Depending on how freshly picked the plantains are, you may notice a sort of cloudy white sap as you cut the skin. Wear gloves or rub some vegetable oil on your hands to protect them, especially if you have sensitive skin.

'Heat or flavour?' asked the lady at the market in Castries, St. Lucia, as I inquired about the homemade pepper sauces she was peddling at her stall. To the untrained palate, all Caribbean pepper sauces will manifest a level of heat. But truly good ones have the right balance of heat and flavour. It's the type of combination that gets you salivating with just one whiff."

Piquant Green Mango Chutney

Any trip to Trinidad and Tobago means sourcing out the best Doubles in Port of Spain. And I usually arrive with a severe craving! I've come to learn that the Doubles vendors are not only judged on the size, texture and taste of their version of the famed street food but also on the chutney and other accompanying hot sauces they provide. Without that "good pepper", an excellent Doubles could easily go unnoticed.

Mango Chutney not only goes great with Doubles but also with everything from scrambled eggs to a juicy T-bone steak! As a matter of fact, you can use this spicy sauce as a side with just about everything for which you would normally use hot sauce. It really opens up your appetite!

You'll Need...

- 1 scotch bonnet pepper (or habanero)
- 2 cloves garlic
- 1/4 teaspoon salt
- 2 green mangoes
- Juice of 1 lime or lemon
- 2 tablespoons shado beni, chopped

Slice the pepper and garlic to make it easier to crush. Using a mortar and pestle,

crush the salt, hot pepper and garlic to a fine paste.

Wash and peel the mangoes. Grate one onto a plate or in a bowl. Remember that the mango will have a pit, so you'll have to work around it. Dice the remaining mango, removing the pit.

In a bowl, combine the pepper-garlic paste, mangoes, lime juice and chopped

shado beni. Give it a good mix. Check to see if more salt is required.

Textures: Traditionally, Mango Chutney is grated. But I like a bit of texture that's why I grate one of the mangoes and dice the other, as if I were making a salsa. It makes a great combination.

Spicy Cucumber Chutney

Cucumber Chutney is one of those spicy condiments that may very well be native to Trinidad and Tobago, especially when it comes to Doubles. A truly good Doubles will always be topped with Cucumber Chutney or, depending on the season, Green Mango Chutney. The sour or tart base, spiced with shado beni and the vibrant heat of scotch bonnet pepper can cause serious drooling—wipe your beak. As with many of the delicacies we enjoy in the Caribbean, we never give much thought to how simple it is to make.

blender or mortar and pestle to give this a really fine chop. Into your device, squeeze lemon juice, add salt, black pepper, shado beni, garlic and scotch bonnet pepper, and rough chop. Start with a few quick pulses then let it run until you have a fine puree. The scent of the lemon juice with the garlic, shado beni and scotch bonnet pepper will be divine and cause you to salivate.

Add the puree into the bowl containing the shredded cucumber and give it a good mix. The idea is to marry all the flavours so you have a balanced Spicy Cucumber Chutney. Allow this to chill in the fridge for a couple hours and you're good to go.

Kick It Up: Add a dash of cumin. Also, I use scotch bonnet pepper but you're free to use habanero or any hot pepper you have on hand or particularly enjoy.

Make It Easy: I use seedless English cucumber so I don't have to remove any seeds. Additionally, I don't remove the skin, as I like the texture and contrast it gives to the chutney. If you opt for cucumbers with seeds, use a spoon to remove them and any soft areas. It must be firm for easy grating.

Storage: This chutney will last in the fridge for at least a week and goes well with anything normally complemented by spicy condiments—even your scrambled eggs during breakfast.

You'll Need...

- 1 large cucumber
- 2 cloves garlic
- 2 tablespoons shado beni
- 1 scotch bonnet pepper
- Juice of 1 lemon
- 1/2 teaspoon salt
- 1/4 teaspoon black pepper

Wash and cut the cucumber into 2 pieces to make it easier to handle. Grate with a box grater, using the side that gives you a shredded finish. Place shredded cucumber into a strainer and squeeze out as much liquid as possible. Place it into a bowl and set aside.

Give the garlic, shado beni and scotch bonnet pepper a rough chop so it will be easier to puree. You can use a compact blender, food processor, regular-sized

Shado Beni Garlic Sauce

I would assume that the foods brought by immigrants from the Middle East to the Caribbean's shores all those years ago sparked our love affair with garlic sauce (like garlic aioli). Over the years—with the addition of shado beni and, in some instances, a little bit of scotch bonnet pepper—it's evolved into a true Caribbean-style condiment.

You'll be blown away by the delightful difference this Shado Beni Garlic sauce makes as a topping for grilled meats, dip for fresh cut fries, condiment for your hamburgers, and a replacement for mayonnaise in sandwiches and wraps. This sauce is quickly making its way into the culinary framework of the Caribbean and versions can be found on just about every island.

creamy and taking on the basic consistency of a runny mayo.

Add the roughly chopped shado beni to the blender. Give it just a few pulses, as you want to be able to see tiny specks of shado beni in the finished product. If you want a little kick, don't hesitate to add a bit of chopped scotch bonnet pepper to the blender as well.

Place the sauce in a sealed container and store in the fridge. Be sure to give it a good shake before serving.

History Lesson: Did you know that the last group of immigrants to venture to colonial Trinidad originated in the region previously known as Greater Syria, which comprises of present day Iraq, Syria, Palestine and Lebanon? Many of the Lebanese hailed from the villages of Buhandoun and Amyoun, while the Syrians came from villages in the Valley of the Christians. These Arabs immigrated to the Caribbean from as early as 1904 in an attempt to escape religious persecution and economic hardship in their native countries.

A Dash Of Something Extra: Taste for salt and add more sugar if you're looking for a creamy garlic finish with a slightly sweet undertone.

You'll Need...

- 10 cloves garlic
- 1/2 cup white wine vinegar
- 1 teaspoon honey (optional)
- 3 1/2 teaspoons white sugar
- 3/4 teaspoon sea salt
- 1/2 cup extra virgin olive oil
- 1/4 cup shado beni, roughly chopped

Place the garlic, vinegar, honey, sugar and salt into a blender or food processor, and puree on high for 1 minute. With the blender still on, in a steady stream, drizzle in the olive oil. The mixture will start going

Blazing Mango-Peach Hot Sauce

Not only will you find variations of explosive hot sauces from island to island, you'll find a unique recipe in just about every home as well. Over the years, I've been experimenting with different ingredients to create some tantalizing hot sauces. This Blazing Mango-Peach Hot Sauce is just me being creative and using what's around me. Don't be fooled by this hot sauce's wonderful fruity fragrance; it is like rocket fuel. I refer to it as the intersection where the Caribbean and Canada collide!

simmer and cook for about 20 minutes, stirring occasionally. The idea is to gently cook the peppers and infuse the sauce with the goodness of the peaches, garlic, cilantro and mango juice. You'll notice that everything will go a bit pale as it cooks. That's totally normal.

After 20 minutes of cooking, remove from the heat and allow the mixture to cool so you don't risk getting burned if it splatters while you're transferring to your food processor or blender. Once cooled, add to food processor or blender, give it a few pulses to start then blend for a minute or two. Try not to over-blend or it will go frothy and ruin the texture. The hot sauce should be thick, but smooth enough to be placed in a squeeze bottle.

Heat Control: I use the entire peppers, as I like that raw and explosive heat. If you want to tame it a bit, you can discard the seeds and the white membrane surrounding the seeds. That is where the majority of the heat resides.

Safety First: As everything simmers in the saucepan, your kitchen will have a strong scent of cooking peppers. You may need to open the kitchen window or turn on the exhaust fan above your stove.

Storage: Store in the fridge in an airtight container for up to six weeks.

You'll Need...

- 10 scotch bonnet peppers (or habanero)
- 1/2 cup cilantro, chopped
- 1 cup mango nectar or juice
- 1 cup canned peaches (with syrup)
- 3/4 teaspoon salt
- 2 cloves garlic
- 1 teaspoon mustard powder
- 1/4 cup vinegar

Wearing gloves when handling the hot peppers, as they can cause problems for sensitive skin, remove their stems, wash and drain. If you don't have gloves, coat your hands with some vegetable oil. Give the peppers a rough chop and, after washing it, do the same for the cilantro. Then place all ingredients in a deep saucepan.

Bring to a boil then reduce to a gentle

Orange-Pineapple Pepper Sauce

Ever ask yourself, "What's with the Caribbean's love affair with pepper sauce and heat?" I'm sure not everyone from the Caribbean is into the hot stuff, but a good majority of us are and we're influencing many people across the globe with the recipes we share.

a rough chop to reduce the work for your blender or food processor. Wear gloves and remember to have your kitchen windows open, as the peppers are very hot and blending them may cause you to choke.

All you need to do now is add all the ingredients to the food processor and give it a few pulses to start. If, like me, you are using canned pineapple chunks, add the syrup in which the pineapple is packed. Continue to pulse until you have a smooth consistency.

When you've achieved a smooth consistency, add the mixture (be careful when pouring it) to a deep saucepan and, on medium heat, bring it up to a boil. Reduce to a gentle simmer and cook for about 10 minutes. For an even smoother consistency, you can return it to your food processor or blender and pulse it again. Try not to go past 30 seconds-1 minute or you'll risk it going frothy.

Storage: This pepper sauce can be stored in the refrigerator for about six to eight weeks. You may find that you need to give it a shake before using, and it will lose some of its kick over time.

Quality: I use store-bought orange juice. Get the good stuff that has no pulp, but is nice and thick.

Safety First: Remember to use caution when handling scotch bonnet peppers, as they are very hot. If you can't source scotch bonnet peppers, first complain to your grocer and then use habanero peppers. They are just as deadly.

You'll Need...

- 15 scotch bonnet peppers
- 1 1/2 cups orange juice
- 3/4 teaspoon salt

- 1 tablespoon brown sugar
- 1 cup pineapple chunks
- 1/4 teaspoon allspice

Wash and give the scotch bonnet peppers

Not Your Mom's Traditional Pepper Sauce

Since my daughter Tehya and I can't get enough of the stuff, I came up with this recipe to mimic the thick garlic hot sauce I get at one of my favourite Thai/Vietnamese restaurants. There's no two ways about it (singing my own praises here), this chunky garlicky pepper sauce is absolutely delightful and will appeal to the Caribbean palate and those who love flavoured heat.

You'll Need...

- 18-25 bird's eye peppers
- 5 scotch bonnet peppers
- 6 cloves garlic
- 2 tablespoons parsley, chopped
- 1 scallion
- 1 cup vinegar
- 3/4 teaspoon salt
- 1/4 teaspoon white sugar
- 2 shado beni leaves
- 1 lemon or lime, peeled and de-seeded
- 1 shallot

Give the ingredients a rough chop to reduce the work your food processor or blender will have to do. If you don't have a food processor or blender, you'll have to use some elbow grease and finely chop everything.

Place all the ingredients into your food processor and pulse. However, be careful not overwork or the sauce will lose its unique chunky texture.

Store in a sealed glass container and if you can ignore temptation, allow it to marinate for a few days before use. You'll be well rewarded. Speaking of storage, the sauce can be left in the fridge for up to three months, but it will lose some of its sting over time.

Kick It Up: You can add more scotch bonnet peppers for extra kick! Additionally, entire ripe limes (with seeds removed) will create a wonderful citrus flavour.

Safety First: Wear gloves when making this pepper sauce and remember to wash your hands with soap and water immediately after.

Share the Heat: Shop around for unique glass containers because this would make a wicked Christmastime gift for someone who loves heat.

Tamarind BBQ Sauce

One of my first memories of tamarind is sucking on fresh-off-the-tree pieces. It had a wicked punch of sour that caused your taste buds to go into immediate shock. For those of you in North America, it's similar to the sour candy you enjoyed as kids.

I updated my childhood memories with this Tamarind BBQ Sauce. Not only will it give you the satisfaction of knowing you made your own BBQ sauce, but you'll also have the tastiest Tamarind BBQ Sauce ever.

You'll Need...

- 1 large onion
- 1 scotch bonnet pepper
- 3/4 cup tamarind pulp
- 1 1/2 cups boiling hot water
- 1 tablespoon olive oil
- 1/2 teaspoon black pepper
- 1/2 teaspoon ground allspice
- 1/4 cup packed brown sugar
- 1/4 cup cider vinegar
- 2 cups ketchup
- 1/4 cup Worcestershire sauce
- 2 tablespoons molasses
- 2 tablespoons yellow mustard
- 1/2 teaspoon salt
- 1 tablespoon ginger, grated
- 1 tomato, diced

Wearing gloves because the pepper may irritate sensitive skin, finely dice the onion and scotch bonnet pepper. Discard the seeds of the pepper if you're concerned about explosive heat. Set aside.

Put tamarind into a bowl and top with the hot water. This will allow you to break down the tamarind into concentrated liquid form. Let sit.

In a deep saucepan over medium, heat the olive oil and add diced onion. Turn your heat to low and cook for 5 minutes, stirring. Add the black pepper and allspice. This will toast the spices and release their flavours. Cook for 1-2 minutes then start adding everything else, except the tamarind, into the pot.

Increase your heat to medium. Bring to a gentle boil and keep stirring. As this comes to a boil, the water with the tamarind pulp should be cool enough for you to handle.

Using a fork, break up the tamarind pulp then get in with your fingers and massage it. This action will release the pulp and the water will become tamarind concentrate. Discard as many of the solids (seeds and fibres) as you can.

Strain the liquid into the pot with the other ingredients and give it a good stir.

Turn the heat up and bring to a boil. Then turn down to a very gentle simmer. The idea is to cook this very slowly so that all the flavours marry and form a tasty sauce. Typically after 30 minutes, it will be finished. If you want a thicker sauce, allow it to cook 45 minutes. Remember, however, that the sauce will thicken up a bit when it cools.

A Dash Of Something Extra: You can add some cinnamon and fresh herbs to personalize this Tamarind BBQ Sauce.

Think Beyond The Grill: This sauce is not only meant for grilling. It also makes a wicked dipping sauce for chicken fingers and is a great topping for burgers.

Storage: Stored in a glass container in the fridge, the sauce will keep for a few months. It won't last that long though, trust me.

Classic Jamaican Jerk Marinade

I just love the variety of exciting and scrumptious food you can find up and down the Caribbean islands. If one dish stands out when you think of Caribbean cuisine, it has to be jerk. Beware, once you give this Classic Jamaican Jerk Marinade a try, you won't go back to the bottled stuff from the grocery store.

By the way, if you want a Trinidadian touch, you can always include our signature additions: a couple shots of rum (I would use a dark rum), a little shado beni and a drop or two of Angostura bitters.

You'll Need...

- 5 scallions
- 5 sprigs thyme
- 2 scotch bonnet peppers
- 2 cloves garlic
- 1 onion
- 2 teaspoons salt
- 1/2 teaspoon black pepper
- 1 tablespoon brown sugar
- 2 teaspoons ground allspice
- 1 teaspoon nutmeg
- 1 teaspoon cinnamon
- 1/3 cup soy sauce
- 2 tablespoons vegetable oil
- 1/4 cup vinegar
- 1/2 cup orange juice
- 1 teaspoon ginger, grated

Rough chop the scallions, thyme, hot peppers, garlic and onion to make them easier to puree, and place in a food processor. Add all the other ingredients and pulse to start then run the puree speed for 2-3 minutes, until everything breaks down to a smooth consistency.

For best results, use this sauce immediately. Marinate your meat for at least 2 hours before grilling or roasting in the oven.

Quantities: If you're using dried thyme, use about 1/2 tablespoon.

Storage: This recipe makes about three cups of marinade, which can be stored in an airtight container in the fridge for one month.

Safety First: When working with hot peppers, wear gloves because the natural oil is deadly.

Heat Control: Most of the pepper's heat is within the seeds and the membrane that surrounds the seeds. To control the heat, discard those. However, for that authentic Jamaican feel, keep the entire pepper.

Caribbean-Creole Sauce For Fish And Grilled Meats

As you know, when I create a recipe I employ the traditional way of making the dish as my base and add my own little touches. So, you'll find that in this Caribbean-Creole Sauce recipe there may be a few foreign ingredients that a typical Creole sauce would not have.

This Caribbean-Creole sauce is excellent on fish (fried, baked, poached, grilled) and on grilled meats.

- 1 teaspoon Worcestershire sauce
- 1 bay leaf
- 3 sprigs thyme
- 1 tablespoon butter
- 1 tablespoon tomato paste
- 1/4 teaspoon salt

Start by chopping and dicing the scallions, green pepper, onion, tomato, garlic (finely), celery, parsley and scotch bonnet pepper. Then, on medium, heat the olive oil in a saucepan and add the diced celery, onion and green pepper. Turn the heat to low and let that gently cook for about 8-10 minutes. Everything will be nice and soft, and you'll have a wonderful base for this delicious sauce.

Turn the heat to medium-high and add all the other ingredients, except the chopped parsley. Stir well and bring to a boil then turn down the heat so you have a gentle simmer. Cook for about 25 minutes, with the lid of the saucepan ajar.

Remove the lid and let the sauce cook on medium heat to thicken up a bit. It should only take a few minutes to do so. Remember to fish out the bay leaf and the thyme stems, and discard. Finish off with the chopped parsley.

Make Ahead: You can certainly make this in advance and keep it in a sealed container in the fridge for at least a week. Just heat and serve when you're ready to add a classic Creole-Caribbean flavour to your dishes.

You'll Need...

- 2 scallions
- 3/4 cup green bell pepper
- 1 medium onion
- 1 large tomato
- 3 cloves garlic
- 3/4 cup celery
- 2 tablespoons parsley
- 1/4 scotch bonnet pepper
- 2 tablespoons olive oil
- 1 1/2 cups chicken stock

Haitian Pikliz: The King Of Condiments

It was about 12 years ago in Miami, while waiting to board a cruise ship, that I enjoyed lunch at a Haitian restaurant and my addiction to Pikliz began. The heat from the scotch bonnet peppers, the flavoured vinegar base and the slight crunch from the cabbage, peppers and onion was such a lovely balance. I don't recall the name of the restaurant, but I do know the Pikliz was served with Griot (fried pork). It was a delightful combination. The hand-painted murals on the walls of the restaurant also stick out in my memory. Today, my daughter Tehya and I use this pickled condiment on burgers, hot dogs or even as a side when we're eating our favourite Caribbean dishes.

You'll Need...

- 2 cups cabbage, shredded
- 1 large carrot, julienned
- 1 cup different coloured bell pepper, thinly sliced
- 1 onion, thinly sliced
- 2 scallions, chopped
- 6 scotch bonnet peppers, thinly sliced
- 4 cloves garlic, thinly sliced
- 12-14 peppercorns
- 4 cloves
- 1 teaspoon salt
- 2 cups vinegar
- Juice of 1/2 lime

Place all prepped ingredients, except for the vinegar, salt and lime juice, in a large bowl. Toss or mix everything together then place in a fairly large glass container with a lid. Top with the salt then pour in the vinegar (to cover everything) and squeeze in the lime juice.

Seal, give the container a good shake and allow it to marinate. I have to warn you that after one whiff, you'll be tempted to go at it. But you must allow it to marinate for about 5 days, as the process will heighten the overall flavours.

Kick It Up: If you like a lot of kick, add more scotch bonnet peppers

Labour of Love: Rather than using a processor, I would recommend testing your knife skills while prepping the ingredients. You'll have a lot more control with the size of the shredding and slicing compared to getting help from a processor.

Although they are much loved, the Caribbean has much more to offer than Rum and Coke or Mojitos. Admittedly, we've mastered the art of making (and enjoying) good rum, but it's also common for 'Ink' (Johnnie Walker Blue) and many fine Scotch, brandies and other liquors to be served at all-inclusive fetes (parties). Wine from every corner of the globe is also making its way onto our tables when we dine out with friends."

Peanut Punch
(for two)

Peanut Punch is one of those drinks that we tend to associate with sexual prowess in the Caribbean. It's said to be good for "the back". All I know is that in high school I used to have it in drink boxes and I could easily drink a full glass everyday. My favourite memory of Peanut Punch, other than the Tetra Paks in which my mom would pack my lunches, is going to visit my godfather at his "chinee" shop in Southern Trinidad's Princes Town. He had Peanut Punch in a sort of fountain machine that contained all the freshly-made drinks. His fruit punch was also deadly! You'll be amazed at the simplicity, quickness and delicious taste of this drink.

You'll Need...

- 8-10 ice cubes
- 2 tablespoons chunky or smooth peanut butter
- 1 cup milk
- 1 tablespoon sweetened condensed milk

Place the ice in a blender first. This way, the condensed milk and peanut butter will go on top of it and not settle on the bottom, where the blades cannot reach.

Add the peanut butter, followed by the milk and condensed milk. Blend for about 30-40 seconds until everything breaks down and is evenly incorporated. You'll have a very creamy and frothy drink that is also filling.

Serve immediately to make sure that ice you crushed doesn't melt.

Personalize: Once you've made traditional Peanut Punch, you can experiment a bit by adding a dash of vanilla essence or nutmeg, a ripe banana, a drop of honey or some granola. I would suggest adding one or two to start and going from there.

A Lively
Carrot Punch

Carrot Punch is one of those rich and creamy drinks you'll find throughout the region. Recipes may differ, but the freshly grated or processed carrot base is constant. On a hot Caribbean day, chilled with a few cubes of ice, this drink is both filling and very refreshing. If you're impatient like me and can't wait for it to chill in the fridge, you can drop in a few cubes of ice and enjoy!

This recipe makes enough Lively Carrot Punch for about eight people.

You'll Need...

- **3 lbs carrots**
- **6 cups water**
- **1/4 teaspoon cinnamon**
- **1/4 teaspoon nutmeg, finely grated**
- **1 teaspoon vanilla**
- **1 can sweetened condensed milk**

Wash and peel the carrots. Peeling with a potato peeler causes a lot of waste so, under cool running water, scrape them with a knife.

Separate the carrots into two batches and place half, along with half of the water, in a food processor or blender. On high speed, process for a few minutes or until you have pureed pulp. Empty the carrots into a large bowl and repeat with the other batch. The alternative is to go old school, as my dad would, and use a box grater.

Using a fine strainer or cheesecloth, strain the liquid from the pulp into another bowl. Then, squeeze the remaining pulp to get out every drop of juice. If you use cheesecloth, you'll find that you can wring out a lot more juice than if you just use your hands. Give the juice another strain to remove any remaining pulp.

To spice things up and sweeten the punch as is traditionally done, whisk in the cinnamon, nutmeg and vanilla. Pour in the sweetened condensed milk, starting off with half a can and adding more as needed—I typically use the entire can. Whisk well, chill and serve.

Big People Only: To serve Carrot Punch as a grown-folk cocktail, add a few shots of rum to the mix.

Refreshing Spiced Caribbean Sorrel

When my daughters were younger, anyone who visited us from the Caribbean always had a few bottles of Sorrel Shandy in their suitcase for them. Indy felt especially grown up drinking from what looked like a beer bottle. My memories of Sorrel—the drink, not the salad greens—are ones of much joy, especially since it's a drink most people from the Caribbean associate with the holiday season. In their garden, my mom and dad would always plant sorrel between their corn and pigeon peas. During the later part of the year, the flowers, which are used for making the drink, would be in full bloom and ready for harvesting.

Strain the contents into a juice jug and add more sugar, as needed.

You can store Sorrel in the fridge for about a week. That is, if you don't finish it before then.

A Dash Of Something Extra: You can certainly add more cinnamon and cloves if you want to give the Sorrel a more "spiced" flavour. If memory serves me correctly, my dad also puts in some dried orange peel during the boiling process.

Dry Works: In the recipe, I use dried sorrel, which is commonly available in most West Indian and some Asian markets.

Big People Only: If you want a grown-up version, add a shot or two of dark rum or vodka to your glass.

Concentrate: If you use less water and omit the sugar that is used in the recipe, you can make concentrated syrup. This can be bottled and kept in the fridge for quite a while. When you're ready for the refreshing taste of Sorrel, pour some into a glass, add sugar and water, and you're good to go. It's perfect for a hot day.

You'll Need...

- 8 cups water
- 2 cups dried sorrel
- 1 teaspoon ginger, grated
- 1 stick cinnamon
- 2 cups sugar
- 4 cloves

In a large saucepan, bring the water to a boil, add all the ingredients and reduce the heat to a rolling boil. Allow this to boil for about 5 minutes.

Turn off the heat, cover the pot and let the mixture steep for at least 4 hours or overnight, which would be best.

Guinness Punch: How We Do Guinness In The Caribbean

Guinness Punch is one of those "big people" drinks we enjoy in the Caribbean—and it's rumoured to give you extra energy and vitality in the bedroom. I'm sure as you make your way up and down the Caribbean islands, you'll find variations of this recipe. So, use this one as a base and feel free to give it your own personal touch. Include some vanilla ice cream or maybe an egg. I'm sure some freshly grated orange zest would also add even more pizzazz. Either way, Guinness Punch is so easy and quick to put together that it will become one of your go-to drinks when you're looking for a little excitement in your life.

You'll Need...

- 1 cup ice
- 1 bottle Guinness
- 1 cup evaporated milk
- 3/4 cup 2% milk
- 8 tablespoons sweetened condensed milk
- 2 drops Angostura bitters
- Pinch nutmeg
- Pinch cinnamon

All you have to do is place all the ingredients in a blender, give it a good pulse and you're good to go.

Remember to not overfill your blender or risk it overflowing as you blend. The idea is to have a rich, creamy drink with a lovely sweet undertone. Serve immediately for best results.

The Beer Out Here: For this recipe, bottled Guinness is better suited than its canned equal, as I find it less frothy. The canned version has that "widget" for making it more draught-like, thus causing the foamy consistency.

Personalize: You may need to adjust the amount of condensed milk to your liking.

If you've never lived on the islands, the Caribbean may evoke daydreams of sipping a cold glass of Rum Punch, decorated with slices of fresh fruit, while taking in the rays on a white sandy beach or at an all-inclusive resort's swim-up bar. Truth be told, Rum Punch is not as common a drink with locals as you would think. More traditional drink choices include Rum and Coke, Pina Colada or even Shandy.

You'll Need...

- 1 cup lime juice, freshly squeezed
- 2 cups grenadine syrup
- 2 cups Caribbean rum
- 1 cup coconut rum
- 2 cups pineapple juice
- 2 cups orange juice
- 5-8 drops Angostura bitters
- Dash nutmeg
- Orange and pineapple slices, to garnish

The only real work here is to squeeze the limes for that freshly squeezed juice you need. Once you do that, add all remaining ingredients into a large container, mix well and put in the fridge to chill.

For that extra zing, you can also add 1 cup of carbonated water to the mix before serving. Pour into your serving jug or punch bowl, add some ice and remember to garnish with slices of orange to make everything look pretty. Then, watch your guests hover around as they enjoy the Ultimate Caribbean Rum Punch. Speaking of punch bowls, I recall my mom having one but to this day I've never seen any punch in that thing. My dad used it for tossing receipts and other things from his pocket, while the rest of us tossed our house keys into it.

Pour It Up: You'll get about 10 cups of rum punch from this recipe and more if you add the carbonated water and ice.

Throw Away Tradition: The traditional way of making rum punch is to use strong white rum but I much prefer dark rum, as I love the undertones you get from it. Also, if you don't have grenadine, use simple syrup or cane juice syrup.

On Christmas morning, with yampee (eye crusties) still in my eyes, I would head to the kitchen for a thick slice of Black Rum Cake and other treats. The ritual was akin to a child from another country scrambling to see what was waiting for him under the Christmas tree. Mom made magic happen in the oven with baked treats, and the holiday season was like my personal foodie heaven."

After TV personality Andrew Zimmerman raved about the Bake and Shark sandwiches he gobbled down on Maracas Beach in Trinidad, requests on CaribbeanPot.com for this recipe became overwhelming. If you're intimidated by making the Fried Bake dough, this recipe will show you how simple it is and how easily you can master it. By the way, these may also be known as Fry Roti, Floats and Fried Dumplings.

The Fried Bake for Bake and Shark is the perfect partner for the Fried Shark on page 91.

You'll Need...

- 3 cups all-purpose flour
- 1/2 teaspoon instant yeast
- 1/4 teaspoon salt
- 1 tablespoon margarine (or butter)
- 1 tablespoon vegetable shortening
- 1 teaspoon baking powder
- 1 1/4 warm cups water
- 3 cups vegetable oil

In a large bowl, place the flour, yeast, salt, margarine, shortening and baking powder Use your hands to mix and break up the margarine and shortening. Once it takes on the consistency of peas, start adding water and form into a dough. It will take about 5 minutes of kneading to form a smooth dough, and you can also use your stand mixer or food processor.

Dust the top of the dough with some flour. Cover the bowl with a piece of plastic wrap, making it airtight, and place it in a warm corner of your kitchen. Allow it to rest for about 45 minutes.

Pull apart the dough into 5 equal, tennis ball-sized balls. After you smooth them out, place the balls on a parchment-lined cookie sheet and cover with a kitchen towel to rest for another 15 minutes. While dough is resting, set up a station with a frying pan containing vegetable oil and a draining basket lined with paper towels.

Rub a little vegetable oil on your work surface (you won't be using a rolling pin)

and place down one of the dough balls. Rub some vegetable oil on your fingers and, working from the centre out, start to stretch the dough while pressing to form a 6-inch in diameter circle.

Heat the vegetable oil on medium-high and gently add a formed Bake to the pan. Remember to place it away from your body so the hot oil doesn't splatter. As soon as it hits the oil, be prepared to flip the Bake so it fries and shapes evenly. Allow to fry for about 3 minutes, flipping a couple times. You're looking for a crispy surface and a golden colour.

Fish out of the pan and place on paper

towels to drain off excess oil. Repeat until all dough is fried. Once slightly cooled, slice open and stuff with the fried shark.

Healthy Combo: To make Bake a bit healthier, you can certainly use a combination of whole-wheat and all-purpose flours.

Not A One-Trick Pony: You can also stuff Fried Bake with Saltfish Buljol (see recipe on page 80) or any of your favourite Caribbean dishes. I like ripping these and eating them with curry dishes as well.

Sada Roti

It's a common misconception that Sada Roti is difficult to make. People avoid even trying. Here's a recipe that proves it's simple and only takes about 30 minutes. You can even cheat and use a food processor to prepare the dough.

a couple minutes on each side, flipping with the help of a spatula since it will be hot. You'll notice 3 things as it cooks: It will increase in thickness, it will start going slightly brown and it will develop air pockets. Once the latter happens, it's time to "swell" the roti, which just means creating huge air pockets.

There are 2 ways to "swell" the roti. The traditional way is to shift the tawa away from the burner so only half the tawa is directly over the flame then, in a circular motion, move the roti over the direct flame. Half the roti should be on the tawa and half over the flame. You'll notice that the process will create an air pocket. If while using this method you notice that only a part of the roti swells, press gently on the roti and the air pocket will move throughout the entire thing.

There is, however, an easier and foolproof way to swell the roti. After you've cooked it on both sides for a couple minutes, and it's started to go brown and air pockets have formed, remove it from the heat. Place it in your microwave on a tea towel, to prevent it from sweating on the direct surface. Set the microwave on high and cook for about 30 seconds. You'll be amazed at how fast and perfectly it swells.

You'll Need...

- 2 1/2 cups all-purpose flour
- 1 tablespoon baking powder
- Pinch salt (optional)
- About 1 1/2 cups water

In a fairly large bowl, combine flour, baking powder and salt. Dust your hands with some flour to prevent the dough from sticking to your fingers then start by adding 3/4 of the water as you knead the dough. Add more gradually, being careful not to end up with a soggy dough. The goal is to create a large, smooth dough ball. If you're using a food processor, simply add all the ingredients and combine. It may take about 5 minutes to knead the dough. Once it's kneaded, cover the bowl and allow the dough to rest for about 15 minutes.

Divide into three even balls.

Dust a clean and dry work surface with flour, flatten a dough ball a bit and work the dough with your fingers—as I'm sure you've seen pizza makers do. To avoid sticking, dust with flour again and start rolling with a rolling pin. Flip over, dust with flour and roll again. You're trying to get a circle shape. The diameter should be between 10-12 inches and about 1/4-inch thick. Repeat until all three balls are done.

The traditional way to cook Sada Roti is by using a "tawa". But if you don't have one, you can achieve the same result using a big, non-stick frying pan. On medium, heat the tawa or pan. Using both hands, gently pick up the flattened dough and place on the heated tawa or pan. Allow it to cook

Storage: Wrap roti in a paper towel after cooking. The idea is to prevent it from going hard by keeping it from coming in contact with air. You can store roti, wrapped in paper towels in a resealable bag, in the fridge for a couple of days. Just reheat in the microwave.

Sweet-Spicy-Sour Tambran Balls

If you're not from the Caribbean, you're likely confused. Fret not because "tambran" is just the local way of saying tamarind.

As a kid, especially in primary school, this treat was a favourite of mine. Today, I still search out Tambran Balls whenever I make a trip home or when I go shopping at the local Asian stores. The big difference with the store-bought ones is that they have no real kick and are really tiny. The ones I often ate during recess were as big as ping-pong balls and hot!

You'll Need...

- **1/2 scotch bonnet pepper**
- **2 cloves garlic**
- **2 cups golden brown sugar**
- **8 oz tamarind**
- **3 tablespoons granulated sugar**

In a bowl (or using a mortar and pestle), place the hot pepper, garlic and about 1 teaspoon of the brown sugar (it gives it a bit of grit to achieve a smooth paste). Pound until smooth. Set aside.

Remove the hard outer shell of the tamarind and pull out the "meat". Try to remove the stringy fibres that may be holding the "meat" together. You have two options now: keep or remove the seeds. Break up the "meat" into pieces and add it to the pepper-garlic paste. Add the brown sugar to the mix and give it a good stir.

Using your hands, start forming ping-pong-sized balls. If you find the balls aren't holding well, add about 1 teaspoon of water to the bowl. If, on the other hand, the mixture is too soft and not taking shape, add some more brown sugar. If the room is hot, it may also be hard to shape the Tambran Balls, as the heat from your hands and room temperature will melt the sugar. Place the mixture in the fridge for a few minutes and try again.

Pour granulated sugar on plate and roll the Balls in it to give them the finishing touch.

Choices: You can always buy tamarind paste that's already free of seeds and the hard exterior shell. I leave the seeds in my finished Tambran Balls because I find they hold a lot of flavour. As a kid, I liked spitting out the seeds. If you do keep the seeds, remember not to sink your teeth into them or you'll be visiting the dentist—and cussing Chris!

Safety First: You're working with hot peppers, so you may want to wear gloves.

Coconut Bake:
Classic Caribbean Bread

Yes, it's bread. But in the Caribbean we call it "bake" because we try our best to confuse the heck out of people with our food names. If you lived on the islands as a child, you would walk into the house after school and be hit with the lovely aroma from the baking action that was taking place in the oven. Immediate hunger would set in because that fresh baking bread smell had a way of getting the best of us. With Coconut Bake, you timed yourself to be around when it came out of the oven so you could have a piece with butter and/or cheese.

For this recipe, although you can get whole dried coconut, using desiccated coconut will save you some work. Desiccated coconut is coconut meat that has been shredded or flaked and then dried to remove as much moisture as possible. I would recommend soaking it in coconut milk to add some life back into it.

You'll Need...

- 4 1/2 cups all-purpose flour (or bread flour)
- 2 teaspoons quick acting yeast
- 1 tablespoon brown sugar
- 3/4 teaspoon salt
- 1/4 cup butter (or shortening)
- 1/4 cup coconut, grated
- 1 cup coconut milk
- Water (if needed)

To make the dough, you can use a food processor. But, if you are less lazy than me, feel free to use your hands. In the food processor (or bowl) place the flour, yeast, sugar, salt and butter (or shortening), and work until you get a sort of crumbly texture. Give the food processor a final pulse before moving on.

Add the grated coconut and pulse, then start to add the coconut milk to form the dough. You may notice that you need additional liquid. If that is the case, add some water. You're looking for a smooth and firm dough. If you are using a food processor, pulse for 3-5 minutes.

Move the dough onto a floured surface and work it until it is firm and smooth. Cut it into two even pieces and, after re-flouring your surface, use a rolling pin to work both into circular shapes. I try to get mine about 1-inch thick and about 10-12 inches in diameter. Use a fork to prick the surface of the dough a bit (always saw my mom do that) then place onto a parchment paper-lined cookie sheet. Cover dough with plastic wrap and allow it to rest for about 20 minutes.

Preheat your oven to 400 F. Remove the plastic and put the Bakes, still on the cookie sheet, on the middle shelf of the oven. Bake 25-30 minutes or until golden brown. You can always stick a toothpick in the centre and if it comes out clean, that means they are fully baked. Serve warm and get ready for your family to fall in love.

Hops bread is one of those things every Trinbagonian can relate to with some level of passion. For me, it brings back memories of visiting the Chinese bakery next to the WASA office for fresh-out-the-oven Hops bread when I finished playing football (soccer) at Irving Park after school. My friends and I would dig deep into our respective pockets to secure enough coins to get a dozen of these temptingly delicious rolls. We never had enough to purchase cheese or even a drink, but we didn't care. We choked that Hops bread down like voracious pigs!

Speaking of after-school adventures and my love for Hops bread, I absolutely hated being in a taxi after school. During my time on the islands, taxis were shared and sometimes another passenger would ask the driver to stop at the bakery. My belly would be in full chorus and this person would have that delicious smelling bread within reach—torture!

You'll Need...

- **2 tablespoons shortening**
- **2 1/2 cups hot water**
- **8 cups all-purpose flour**
- **1 tsp salt**
- **2 teaspoons granulated sugar**
- **1 pack or 1 tbsp instant yeast**
- **Water**

Stir the shortening into the hot water until it completely melts and the water becomes lukewarm.

In a large bowl, place about 7 cups of the flour, salt, sugar and yeast. Give it a good mix to combine evenly. Start adding water, a little at a time, until you have soggy dough.

Dust a surface with flour and place the dough onto it. Knead for about 5 minutes, adding flour as necessary, until you have a well-formed dough ball that's soft yet firm.

Spray a large bowl with cooking spray, place the dough into it and cover with plastic wrap or a damp kitchen towel. Allow to rise for about 40–50 minutes, depending on how active your yeast is and the warmth of your kitchen. You're looking for it to double in size.

Line a baking sheet with parchment paper or grease and dust with flour. Remove

the plastic wrap and punch the dough to release the air. Divide the dough into 12 even dough balls (about 3 inches in diameter) and set onto the parchment-lined baking sheet. Allow to rise again by placing a damp towel or cloth on top to keep the moisture in and prevent the top of each individual Hops bread dough ball

from drying out. Set aside in a warm corner of your kitchen for 45 minutes.

Preheat your oven to 400 F and set on the middle rack to bake. It will take between 20-25 minutes, depending on your oven, for the Hops bread to be nice and golden.

North American kids eat cereal before heading off to school. On the islands, we grew up drinking tea—which actually meant any hot drink, including coffee, Milo, Ovaltine, chocolate tea, green tea and more. Along with tea, we usually had a slice of cake, sweet bread, crackers or Coconut Drops. It's no wonder that when the scent of Coconut Drops blankets my kitchen now, it brings back a rush of childhood memories. I was one of those kids who actually loved school and looked forward to it.

The true master of these Coconut Drops, as well as Coconut Sweet Bread, was my grandmother. When she passed away at 99, baking was out of the question but she was still the Coconut Drops queen!

You'll Need...

- 1/4 stick (about 4 tablespoons) butter, softened
- 1/2 cup sugar
- 1 large egg
- 1 teaspoon vanilla
- 1/4 teaspoon Angostura bitters
- 3 cups all-purpose flour
- 2 teaspoons cinnamon
- 3 teaspoons baking powder
- About 1/2 cup water
- 1/2 cup raisins
- 1 cup coconut, shredded

Glaze...
- 2 tablespoons sugar
- 1/4 cup water

Add the room temperature butter and sugar to a bowl, and combine. I start off using the back of a large spoon to work the butter-sugar combo against the sides of the bowl, but end by using an electric hand mixer. You're looking for a smooth, creamy texture with no gritty feel of sugar left behind. Pour in the egg, vanilla and bitters, and give it a good whisk.

In a bowl, combine flour, cinnamon and baking powder. Once fully incorporated, add the dry ingredients into the creamed butter to create a dough. It'll be a bit tough to work, so pour in the water. I work the dough manually and sometimes end up using my hands. Fold in the shredded coconut and raisins. With your oven at 350 F, grease a cookie sheet or line it with

parchment paper. Drop batter onto the cookie sheet and bake for about 25-30 minutes or until it starts to turn golden. I do two batches of 12.

While baking, create the glaze by combining water and sugar. Once Drops are done, brush with glaze. You can also sprinkle some sugar over each one for a special touch. Return to the oven for 2-3 minutes.

Throw Away Tradition: Traditionally, fresh grated coconut is used for this recipe. Since I don't have access to the fresh stuff, I settle for the packaged sweetened and shredded coconut. If you have the unsweetened kind, feel free to use that.

Coconut Sugar Cake

This recipe is somewhat refined in comparison to my dad's and, if I may be bold, better than his! He's old school when it comes to making Coconut Sugar Cake, preferring to get fresh dry coconut and doing his thing with the grater. Besides not liking to grate coconut like a mad man (my fingers still show battle scars from my last time), I wanted to prove how quick and simple this recipe can be.

You'll Need...

- 2 cups sugar
- 1 1/2 cups water
- 2 bay leaves
- Thick slice fresh ginger
- 1 teaspoon vanilla essence
- 2 cups unsweetened desiccated coconut
- 4-6 drops red food colouring (optional)

To make the syrup: In a deep saucepan heat the sugar, water, bay leaves and a thick slice of ginger. Bring to a rolling boil and allow to cook (constantly stirring with a spoon or whisk) until it reduces and becomes thick, about 5-7 minutes. Remove the bay leaves and ginger, and discard. If, on the other hand, you like the strong aroma and taste of ginger and bay leaves, you can always grate the ginger and crush the bay leaves into the syrup.

Stirring constantly, add to the vanilla essence and the desiccated coconut to the pan with the syrup. It will require about 7-10 minutes on medium heat to get the consistency you're looking for. The idea is to burn off as much liquid as you can, so you have a thick and sticky texture.

When the coconut mixture starts coming away from the sides of the pan and somewhat clumps, take it as a sign that you're close. Finish off with the drops of food colouring and combine well.

On a parchment-lined cookie sheet, take spoonfuls of the mixture and make small heaps to form Cakes. The Cakes will need time to cool, set and take shape before you can fully enjoy them. Remember, you just made a sugar syrup so it will be extremely hot. Have some patience.

Your kitchen will have the lovely aroma of coconut, vanilla essence, ginger and bay leaf. You'll feel like a big kid when you taste this treat.

Squares: If you have a 1-inch deep pan, you can pour the cooked mixture into it, allow to cool and then cut into even squares.

Taste The Rainbow: Be creative by making different coloured batches and stacking them for a rainbow effect.

Storage: Store in an airtight container for maximum freshness and refrigerate if you plan on saving the Cakes for more than a few days.

Cassava Pone

As many islands in the Caribbean, so too are there recipes for making Pone—as it's lovingly called. In this recipe, I've tried to cover all the basics to give you a mouthwatering Cassava Pone. You can certainly personalize it as you become more experienced.

You'll Need...

- 3 cups sweet cassava, grated
- 1 cup pumpkin, grated
- 1/2 cup coconut milk
- 1 cup brown sugar
- 1 teaspoon cinnamon, ground
- 1/2 teaspoon nutmeg
- 1 cup coconut, grated
- 2 tablespoons butter, melted
- 1 cup evaporated milk
- 1 teaspoon baking powder
- 1 teaspoon vanilla essence
- 1 teaspoon ginger, grated
- 1/2 cup raisins

Peel, wash, and grate the cassava and pumpkin. The skin on both will be tough, so you'll need to use a sharp paring knife or potato peeler. After peeling, it's just a matter of grating both items, which will take a bit of labour. Do watch out for your fingers when the pieces get small. I usually use a piece of paper towel for better grip when handling small pieces.

Before starting this step, preheat your oven to 350 F. Then, in a large bowl, using a wooden spoon or whisk, combine the coconut milk, brown sugar, ground cinnamon and nutmeg. Give that a good whisk to break down the sugar. To this, add the cassava, pumpkin and coconut with the remaining ingredients and stir until well combined.

Using cooking spray or a light coat of butter, grease a baking pan or dish (I use a ceramic pie dish). Pour the batter into the baking dish and place on the middle

rack of the hot oven. Although every oven differs in heat and distribution, you're aiming for one hour of baking. However, if you find that the middle of the Cassava Pone is still wet, or not as firm and golden brown as the edges, allow it to bake an extra 10-20 minutes. Do the toothpick test in the middle of the pone and if it comes out clean, it's fully cooked. The air will be sweet with the lovely aroma of baked goodness. Don't be surprised if your loved ones keep asking, "Is it done yet?"

Tradition vs. Convenience: Some work is required to grate the cassava and pumpkin but you can also use a food processor or purchase already grated cassava from your better-stocked local grocery store. Also, those of us in North America can certainly use pumpkin pie filling. I know it's not traditional but sometimes convenience trumps tradition.

No matter what you call it, Black Cake, Rum Cake or Fruit Cake is well known throughout the Caribbean. And I can bet my last dollar that no two recipes are the same. My grandmother's cake is uniquely different than my mom's and I'm sure my cake is different than theirs.

Before you get to the actual Black Cake recipe (see next page), you must prepare the fruit. It's important for the fruit to soak or marinate for at least a month before it's ready for the Black Cake batter. I even know people who do this step a year in advance.

You'll Need...

- 1 lb pitted prunes
- 2 cups dark rum (a spiced rum is preferable)
- 4 cups Sherry
- 1 lb mixed peel
- 1/2 lb raisins
- 1/2 lb maraschino cherries
- 1/4 lb lemon peel

Start by giving the prunes a rough chop. This will make it easier when you process them and also verify that each prune is truly seedless. If you're old school and want to use a food mill, do your thing.

Put everything into the food processor, and add about a cup or two of the rum and Sherry. Give it a few pulses to get things going then run until you have a thick but smooth consistency. If you'd like to have little bits of the fruit in the cake when it's made, keep an eye on the consistency.

Once pureed, pour the mixture into a large bowl and add the rest of the rum and Sherry. Give it a good stir to make sure the fruit absorbs all the liquor. Once it's combined, place the mixture into a container that can be sealed. I use a glass bottle. This can be stored in any cool, dark spot in your kitchen or pantry for a year.

Refer to Caribbean Black Cake Part 2 on page 152 for making the dough and baking the cake.

Tradition vs. Convenience: Traditionally, cherry wine or cherry brandy (an alcoholic drink unique to the Caribbean) is used along with rum. I use Sherry instead since it is the only option available to me. In all honesty, the Sherry gives the cake a wonderful rounded fruity flavour, which I quite like.

Reverse It: If you prefer, you can soak the fruit without pureeing and do that step the day you're actually making the cake. However, I find that not only is it more convenient to have this step done in advance, but the fruit seems to absorb all that rum flavour and goodness much better when everything is pureed. By the way, this recipe will produce enough mixture for you to have leftovers, so simply keep it in your pantry for next time.

Caribbean Black Cake: Part 2

This Black Cake recipe takes me back to my childhood, as my siblings and I always assisted my mom in making a few of these cakes the night before Christmas. Besides the scent of freshly painted walls, varnished floors, and new curtains and bed sheets, which were all part of preparing the house for the holidays, the tempting fragrance out of the oven leading up to and including Christmas Day is one of pure joyful memories for me.

You'll Need...

- 2 sticks (about 1/2 lb) unsalted butter (room temperature)
- 1 cup brown sugar
- 6 large eggs (room temperature)
- 1 teaspoon vanilla
- Dash Angostura bitters (optional)
- 1 teaspoon mixed essence
- 1 teaspoon lime zest, grated
- 4 1/2 cups fruit, pureed and soaked
- 2 cups all-purpose flour
- Pinch salt
- 1 teaspoon cinnamon
- 1/4 teaspoon nutmeg, freshly grated
- 1/8 teaspoon allspice
- 2 teaspoons baking powder
- 1 tablespoon browning

Using a stand mixer, cream the butter and

sugar until you have a fluffy and smooth consistency. If you don't own a stand mixer, add the sugar and butter into a large bowl and use a hand mixer. Back in the old days, it was my dad's job to do this with a large spoon. Mr. Man was old school.

After you have a smooth and fluffy batter base, add the eggs, one at a time, and mix thoroughly.

Add the vanilla, bitters, mixed essence and lime zest, and give it a good mix. If you're using a hand mixer, add the soaked fruits in two batches, working them in with a spatula then giving everything a good mix with mixer. Once you complete both batches, you should have a "wet" batter.

In another bowl, sift the flour, salt, cinnamon,

nutmeg, allspice and baking powder.

In 1/3 amounts, three times in total, add the dry ingredients to the wet batter, mixing well between each addition. With the batter completely combined, add the browning and give it final good mix.

You'll have enough batter for 2, round, 10-inch pans. You may also use 3, disposable, rectangle pans. Grease and line them with parchment paper to avoid any issues once the cakes are baked. Pour in batter 2/3 up each pan and place in a preheated 250 F oven for 2 1/2 hours. Since all ovens differ, I suggest you give the cakes the toothpick test after the 2 1/2 hours to see if they're fully baked.

After you remove the cakes from the oven, allow them to cool a bit. Once they've cooled, brush a mixture of rum and Sherry over the cakes and allow it to soak through. This will give them that added kick! Trust meh!

Browning Explained: The browning required to give the cake its dark, rich colour and Caribbean flavour is not your typical gravy browning. It's a Caribbean style burnt sugar browning, which can be sourced at West Indian markets.

Get Cracking: Crack each egg into a small bowl first so you can fish out any shell that may have fallen in. This way, you're not diving in the batter for it.

On the islands, it's common to have banana trees around your home, so we always had a range of banana varieties to snack on. My mom would make this treat for us whenever the bananas were going a bit too ripe. Back then though, there was no confectioners' sugar topping!

You'll Need...

- 3 ripe bananas
- 1 egg
- 1/2 cup sugar
- 1 teaspoon vanilla extract
- 1/2 teaspoon ground cinnamon
- 2 cups all-purpose flour
- 1 tablespoon baking powder
- 3 cups vegetable oil
- **Confectioners' sugar (optional, but nice finishing touch)**

Into a fairly large bowl, peel and cut the bananas into chunks. Using a fork or potato masher, mash to a smooth consistency. It should have the texture of baby food—parents will know what I mean.

In a separate bowl, whip the egg. Add sugar, vanilla and cinnamon then whip again until the sugar breaks down. Add that to the bowl of mashed bananas and combine. You can certainly use an electric mixer, but I prefer a wire whisk to burn off some calories before replacing them with tasty ones.

Slowly start adding the flour and baking powder. Mix until you have a smooth, lump-free batter.

Heat the oil on medium-high and drop in a few tablespoons of batter. It will take about 1 minute for the batter to turn golden-brown. Flip and cook for another minute until the other side is golden-brown. The fritters will float when they're cooked. Repeat until all the batter is used.

Remove from the pan, drain on paper towels, dust with confectioners' sugar and serve warm. The Caribbean-Favourite Banana Fritters go great with a side of vanilla ice cream.

Classic Trinbagonian Coconut Ice Cream

As a kid, the sound of the hand crank ice cream maker (and later, the electric one) was music to my ears. Sunday afternoons, especially when we had family visiting, meant homemade coconut, soursop, barbadine or any fruit that was in season, ice cream. We would circle that ice cream pail like hawks, ready to pounce. The key was listening closely to the hum of the ice cream maker, which makes a dragging sound when the ice cream is firm. That was the cue to attack.

You'll Need...

- **4 cups coconut milk**
- **1/2 cup sugar**
- **4 tablespoons custard powder**
- **2 cups heavy cream**
- **1 can sweetened condensed milk**
- **1 teaspoon vanilla extract**
- **1 can coconut milk**

In a deep pot, over low heat, whisk 1 cup of the coconut milk, sugar, custard powder and heavy cream. Keep whisking, as this can easily start to stick to the bottom of the pot and go lumpy. The goal is to get a thick consistency, which takes between 5-10 minutes. Turn off the stove and add the remaining ingredients to the pot. Whisk like you've never whisked before (or use an electric mixer). It's important to break down any lumps that may form, and to incorporate everything. Place in the fridge to cool for at least an hour.

After it has cooled, place the mixture in your ice cream maker and freeze according to its instructions. I own an electric one that churns with the aid of a small motor. My machine takes about 30 minutes to fully firm the ice cream and, as I mentioned, the machine will start dragging when the ice cream is fully done.

If you like soft serve textured ice cream, you can enjoy as is. However, I like to empty the ice cream into freezer containers and place in the freezer for about 30 minutes to really firm up. This also allows me to keep small batches for when I crave a refreshing dessert.

Tradition: Instead of using coconut milk, the traditional way is to get a couple dried coconuts, husk, grate, add water and squeeze out the milk from the pulp. To save time and sourcing "good" dried coconut, opt for the canned coconut milk.

Grilled Pineapple With Caramel Rum Sauce

Without a doubt, this will become the go-to dessert recipe in your home—as it is in mine. With cinnamon-dusted pineapple grilled to release its natural sugars and juices then simmered in a wonderful brown sugar-rum sauce, it's just…yum! On its own or as a topping for a couple scoops of vanilla ice cream, this grilled pineapple will excite your taste buds.

Can someone please tell me why my mom never made this for my siblings and I even though we had pineapple growing in our backyard? Mom, we need to have a serious chat!

all the flavours blend and you have a consistency with which you're happy. Your kitchen will have the wonderful scent of the brown sugar and grilled pineapple, and the rum will just take this to another level—wicked for days!

Storage: You can store the pineapple in a sealed container, in the fridge, for a week or so. Just microwave to heat every time you're ready to use.

Servings: An average pineapple will give you enough for four people and about eight people as a topping for ice cream.

A Dash Of Something Extra: Top with some toasted coconut flakes, if you want to add more flavour and texture to this wonderful dessert. Additionally, if you're like me and enjoy Rum and Raisin Ice Cream, you can add some raisins to the rum sauce.

Minors Allowed: If you're serving this to minors or you don't deal with alcohol, no worries. All the alcohol burns off during the simmering process, but you do get a wonderful flavour from it.

Tools: I use a stovetop cast iron grill pan for grilling but you can also use your outdoor or indoor grill, or a non-stick frying pan.

You'll Need...

- 1 ripe pineapple
- 1/2 cup dark rum
- 1/2 cup golden brown sugar
- 4 tablespoons butter
- 1/4 teaspoon cinnamon

Prepare the pineapple according to the directions in the "It's Not Just Bananas and Mangoes" section of the book then sprinkle with cinnamon and toss. Brush a grill pan with some vegetable oil or cooking spray and, on medium-high heat, grill the pineapple spears for 3-4 minutes on each side. Try not to over-grill or the pineapple will go soft and lose its shape. Set aside.

In a fairly deep saucepan, add the brown sugar and butter. Cook on medium heat, stirring continuously, until it melts, starts to go a darker colour and turns frothy. This will take about 4-6 minutes.

Turn off the heat and gently pour in the rum. Have a whisk handy, as it will clump and you'll think it's ruined. Fear not and keep stirring. After 2 minutes of stirring, turn the heat back to medium (the alcohol should have dissipated by now) and keep stirring until you have a semi-thick consistency.

Add the grilled pineapple pieces to the pan and gently toss the sauce all over them. Cook for a couple minutes or until

Chris De La Rosa's love of Caribbean cooking has taken him from a small village in Trinidad and Tobago to millions of kitchens around the world, thanks to his website CaribbeanPot.com. Launched in 2009 as a place for the self-taught chef to share his favourite Caribbean dishes and document family recipes for his daughters, the site, which (at the time of printing) had more than 450,000 page views a month, has grown to include a Facebook page of more than 45,000 fans, a newsletter with 36,000 subscribers and a YouTube channel that has amassed about 11 million views.

From the time Chris was just five-years-old, he was already comfortable in the kitchen, thanks to his mother's insistence that he partake in daily chores such as picking fresh herbs from the family garden. Gathering cooking tips from other family members along the way, Chris was well equipped, by the time he moved to Canada in 1989, to fend for himself among the pots and pans. Not limited to Caribbean cooking, Chris also mastered North American fare such as barbecue. However, his heart belonged to the Caribbean recipes on which he was raised.

Modeling CaribbeanPot.com after classic cookbooks, which offer step-by-step instruction and a list of ingredients, Chris began by posting recipes on a weekly basis. Wanting to personalize the site, Chris added anecdotes to the recipes as well as photos for each step in the directions. His YouTube videos and Facebook page offered other dimensions to CaribbeanPot.com, and fans from around the world began to seek out Chris for tips on everything from making the perfect Rice and Peas and Jerk Chicken to braising oxtail in Guinness. With an ever-growing fan base, CaribbeanPot.com quickly solidified itself as a hub that Chris hopes will help to boost the rank of Caribbean cooking to that of French or Italian cuisine.

What's next for the one-stop-shop of Caribbean cooking, recipes and culinary culture? Chris is currently working on a series of cookbooks, the first of which is an e-book entitled, The Vibrant Caribbean Pot: 60 Traditional and Fusion Recipes Vol. 1 and second, which you hold in your hands. He is also interested in hosting a cooking show on local or national TV, submitting recipes to print publications and helping to educate the general public about the evolution of Caribbean cuisine. However, moving CaribbeanPot.com beyond the online realm doesn't just mean serving up tips, and delicious versions of classic and modern bites. Chris also hopes to produce a line of spice blends and hot sauces that will introduce novices to the joys of Caribbean cooking and allow seasoned chefs to elevate the flavours simmering within their own Caribbean pots. ◖

THE WOMEN BEHIND THE BOOK

KAREN NICOLE SMITH

◖ The project manager for CaribbeanPot.com as well as this book has, drawn from her writing and managing background to contribute to Chris' dream. With both of Karen Nicole's parents hailing from Trinidad, working with CaribbeanPot.com takes on a deeper and more personal meaning—not to mention that she adores Doubles with slight pepper.

IZABELA SZYDLO

◖ The editor of "The Vibrant Caribbean Pot" is the National Food and Wellness Editor for Metro English Canada, the country's most read daily newspaper. She has been a journalist and editor for 13 years, and her work has appeared in publications across Canada. As an honourary West Indian, Izabela can't get enough of Trinidadian Pelau and will never turn down Jamaican Festival.

ASHLEY MCKENZIE-BARNES

◖ The art director of the "The Vibrant Caribbean Pot" book, has over 10 years experience as a art director, graphic designer and visual artist. She has worked with high-profile clients such as Sway and The Grid magazines, Yahoo! Canada, Alliance Films, Manifesto Festival of Arts & Culture, and more. She is also the owner of VividBeautyDesigns.com, not to mention a proud Jamaican who lives for Breadfruit with Ackee and Fry Fish.

What started as a means to document recipes for my daughters so they could take with them a piece of our kitchen and warm family memories wherever they landed in the pursuit of education, has turned into something truly global.

Although I grew up surrounded by great cooks, I never envisioned that I would help introduce millions around the world to the Caribbean's rich and diverse cuisine. Those Saturday mornings when my siblings and I took turns in the kitchen with my mom seemed like a chore but truly influenced me as a man and how I approach life. Mom and dad, I'm reminded daily how blessed I am to have you as parents, confidants and role models. Mom, you're still the best in the kitchen and I hope this book is a direct reflection of what you passed onto me.

Though my family calls Canada home, our kitchen reflects a traditional Caribbean one—alive with spices, fresh herbs and exotic ingredients. Thank you to my beautiful wife and best friend, Caron, for giving me full range in the kitchen to do my thing. I truly appreciate your love, support and that you're forever championing my causes. My daughters, Kieana, Tehya and India, no one appreciates my kitchen concoctions more than you. Every time I hear you compliment a dish, say how much you miss my food when you're away from home or when I see you put one of my food pics on Instagram, that's all the motivation I need. Kieana, thanks for always helping me clean up my kitchen messes. Tehya (and Bridget and Lexi), thanks for being my guinea pigs and appearing in my cooking videos. India, my spicy Indy, thanks for keeping me on my toes.

I've had the privilege of learning from people who have mastered the art of traditional Caribbean cooking. Aunt Victoria, you became my second mother when I moved to Canada, and I want to thank you for giving me the gift of curry and influencing many of the Indian dishes I make. Uncle B, Soup Saturdays, will never be the same without you.

A special thanks goes to my sisters, who are some of my biggest supporters. Glenda, your critical nature forces me to perfect whatever I cook and share with you. Tricia, your contribution to my ongoing education is valued. I'm always excited when a package comes in the mail. My brother, Ted, I'm ready to challenge you for the best Trinbago Callaloo. Thanks for setting the bar high.

My friends, Richard, Alleyne and Marko, it's good to know you're always in my corner. We definitely have to take a trip "home" so I can share with you where this all started.

To the three women who are directly responsible for putting this book together, Karen Nicole Smith, Ashley McKenzie-Barnes and Izabela Szydlo, I'm forever grateful for your expertise. Your contributions are immense, without which this would not have become a reality. Special thanks to Karen Nicole; you're such a strong advocate and always challenge me to be the best I can be.

I'd like to also acknowledge the continued support I get from the millions of website visitors, Facebook fans, YouTube viewers, Tweeters and Instagram connections. Without you, none of this would have been possible.

Happy cooking,

Chris De La Rosa

FIND CHRIS DE LA ROSA ONLINE

 ChrisDeLaRosa.com

 CaribbeanPot.com

 Search keyword: CaribbeanPot

 youtube.com/caribbeanpot

 twitter.com/obzokee

 caribbeanpot

●● flickr.com/photos/caribbeanpot/

MOM TOLD YOU TO EAT YOUR VEGGIES.
CHRIS' NEXT BOOK WILL PROVE HER RIGHT.